W9-BVF-206

This edition first published
in 2007
by UNIVERSE PUBLISHING
A Division of Rizzoli
International Publications, Inc.
300 Park Avenue South
New York, NY 10010
www.rizzoliusa.com

Copyright © 2007,
Marvin Scott Jarrett, Nylon LLC

Text by Fiorella Valdesolo
Design by Josh Gurrie

All rights reserved. No part of this book may be reproduced, stored in a retrieval system, or transmitted in any form or by any means, electric, mechanical, photocopying, recording, or otherwise, without prior consent of the publisher.

2007 2008 2009 2010
10 9 8 7 6 5 4 3

Printed in China

ISBN-13:978-0-7893-1539-7
Library of Congress Control Number:
2006906356

Publisher's Note:
Neither Universe Publishing nor NYLON has any interest, financial or personal, in the companies listed in this book. No fees were paid or services rendered in exchange for inclusion in these pages.

PR

TTY

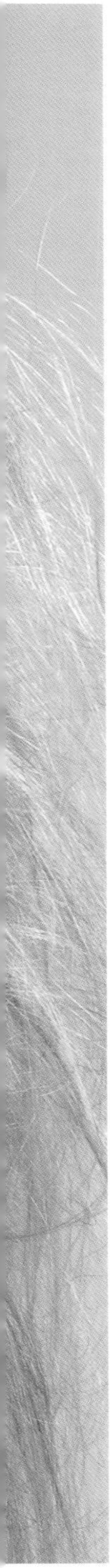

CONTENTS

FOREWORD

Since we started the magazine eight years ago, beauty at *NYLON* has been noticeably different than what you see in other women's magazines. We set out to create a publication that had a singular vision when it came to fashion, entertainment, and music, and beauty was no exception. There are absolutely no how-tos. No deconstruction of celebrity makeup trends. No fat-blasting workout plans. And no boring cheap-versus-pricey product guides. What *NYLON* has offered our readers is a creative, unexpected approach to beauty coverage, with a sense of irreverence. We have made up models as life-size Barbie dolls, found beauty inspiration in everyone from Amy Fisher to David Bowie, and highlighted the most stripped-down and natural all the way up to the most exaggerated, artificial looks there are. And for our beloved (and oft-copied) "Private Icon" feature, we have always looked to legendary beauties of years past to inspire future generations.

At *NYLON*, beauty has always been considered a means of personal expression that says as much about who you are as the clothes you wear do. Just as the girl who opts for heels is a far cry from the one who prefers dunks, the girl who is rocking the perfectly painted red lips is going for something very different than the one whose only beauty statement is the color of her constantly changing Manic-Panicked hair. And *NYLON* has always celebrated both. Consider this book an ode to the beauty of those girls, and everyone in between.

MARVIN SCOTT JARRETT
Editor-in-Chief, *NYLON*

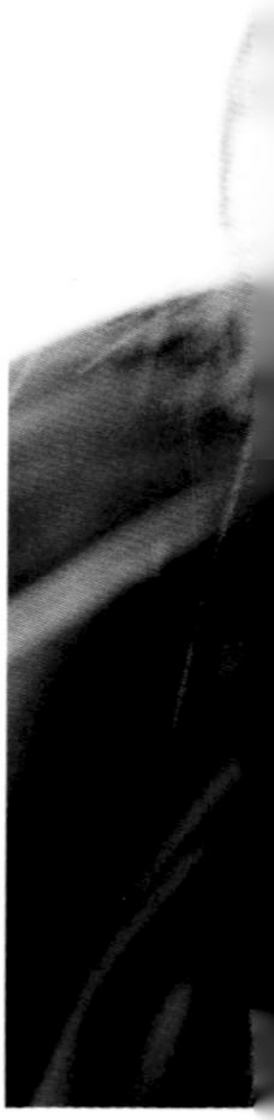

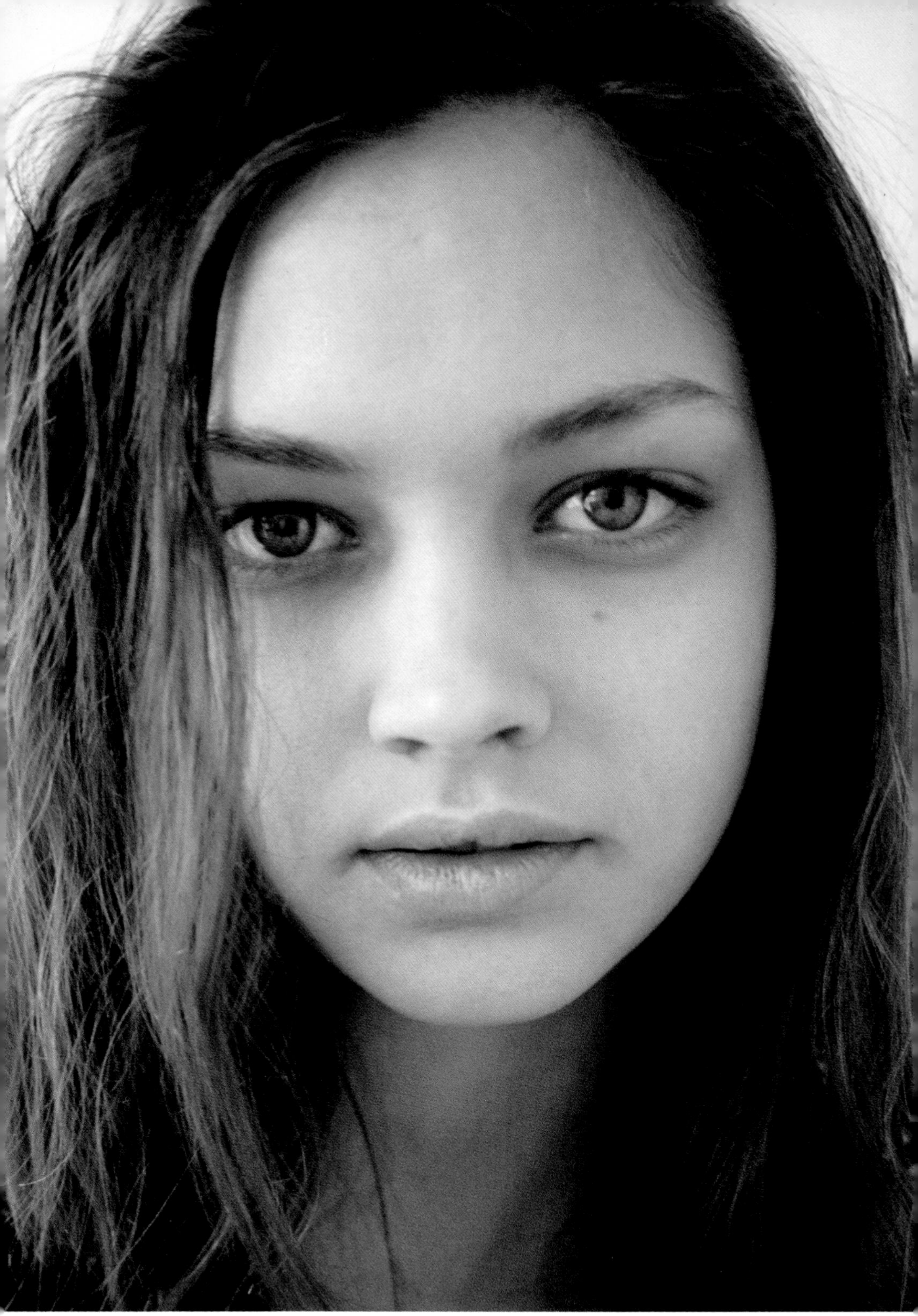

INTRODU

TION

I can't remember the taste of my first kiss. Or the feeling I had gripping my high school diploma. Or the outfit I so fastidiously selected for my very first day at my very first job post-college. What I can recall clearly are the beauty particulars: I doused myself in Exclamation perfume and rolled on sticky, watermelon-flavored gloss in anticipation of that behind-the-gym smooch; for graduation, I henna-ed then fastened tiny braids in my long center-parted hippie-hair; and I overdid it with concealer at work trying valiantly to disguise a monstrous zit on my chin.

More than anything, beauty is evocative. Many details about my Italian grandmother become fuzzy between visits, but what always remains steadfast in my mind is her scent—an inviting fusion of the powdery remnants of her morning application of Chanel N° 5 and the rich spice of meatballs or whatever else she's been whipping up in the kitchen—the velvety soft feel of her skin, and the appearance of her jet-black hair, tightly curled each week into a petrified permanent helmet. While these elements have always remained her signature, my own have changed drastically over the decades. There was the middle school crimped hair, blue eye shadow, and clear mascara. Then the tragic period in junior high school that can only be referred to as "the scrunchie years." The Earth-Mother era, complete with leg fur, patchouli-drenched skin, and hemp hair wraps. The short-lived dalliance with Eurotrash stylings: blond streaks, inflated boobs, gloss, and bronzer. The shorn, spiky hair, a do-rag, and a bindi-face crystal phase whose influences remain grossly unclear. And my current obsession with mirroring the moody panache of French New Wave mademoiselles like Jane Birkin, with ink-colored kohl and a brow-grazing fringe. Each beauty stage can even be pinpointed by my choice of fragrance: Electric Youth (trying to fit in); Anaïs Anaïs (trying to smell like my mom); cK One (trying not to be girly); Kenzo's Parfum d'Été (trying to be unique); Gucci Rush (trying to be sexy); Chanel Allure (trying to be sophisticated); and finally, Vivienne Westwood Boudoir (ah, success). Often, the most memorable beauty moments haven't been the successes, but rather the failures: my painful introduction to the baby-pink Bic razor and the bloody welts that ensued, the unnatural twists and turns of the spiral perm, the Tang-colored mistakes caused by overzealous Sun-In applications, glitter used with a heavy hand in lieu of eye shadow, dark ring-around-the-mouth lip liner, and the Dorothy Hamill-era bowl cut (I blame that one on my mom).

The beauty of, well, beauty at *NYLON* is that these "experiments," both my own and those of women (and men) far more famous than I, are constantly amassed and treasured. Because it is only by relying heavily on the past (and ignoring the current red carpet sea of sameness) that we are able to cull inspiration for the future. There is something infinitely more affecting about Brigitte than Britney. Or Jean (Shrimpton, Harlow, or Seberg, take your pick) rather than Jessica. Or Edie over Ms. Electra. And it is all presented on the pages of *NYLON* with an overarching sense of humor, a biting wit and a lighthearted spirit. Because that's the way beauty should be. The feminist scholar Naomi Wolf famously devoted the entirety of her seminal tome, *The Beauty Myth*, to a dissection of the beauty industry. In Wolf's mind, the industry is merely a trap for women—enticing them with false promises while simultaneously creating impossible ideals for them to live up to. She argued that women feel intense pressure to conform to society's concept of what's beautiful in order to find both success and social acceptance. We say it's time to take beauty back. To claim it as our own! Beauty should be used to celebrate each individual, not as a divisive or exclusionary device. And if this book can be a tool in that regard, that would be, appropriately enough, pretty smart.

FIORELLA VALDESOLO
Beauty Editor, *NYLON*

PART

1 THE ELEMENTS

COUNTER

What makes a product emblematic? Is it based merely on how many are unloaded from counters around the world each day? Partially, yes. But, like with the most beloved actors and musicians of our time, being exemplary goes beyond sales or popularity. A truly emblematic product has to stand the test of time, and remain as desirable today as it was the day it launched. Using that precise gauge, we came up with the following star products from twenty of our favorite cosmetic brands. Each one is just as cherished now as it was at the time it came out.

CULTURE

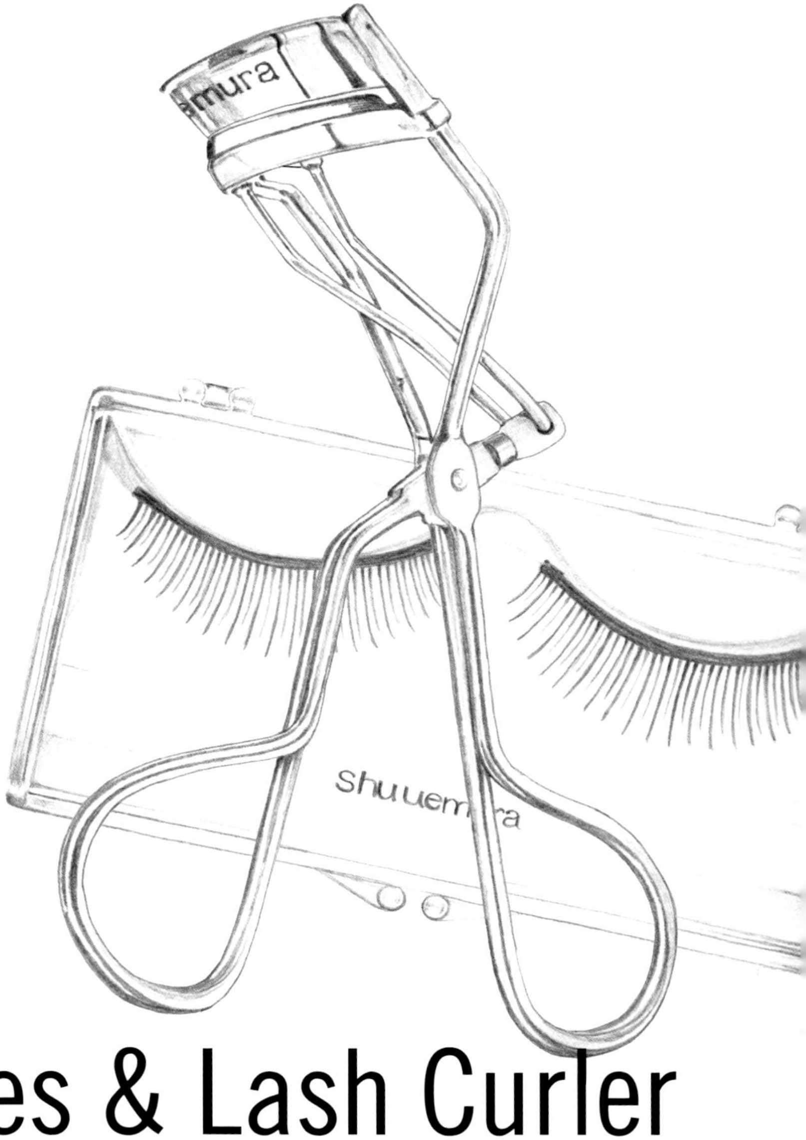

SHU UEMURA

False Lashes & Lash Curler

Many a one-name wonder has relied heavily on the false lash/curler combo. Garbo would not have looked nearly as glamorous in those famous moodily lit black-and-white photos by Horst P. Horst without her extra fringe, her eyelids so heavy they're practically closed. Dietrich used individual lashes at the outer corners of her lids to create a wider space, giving her that signature mysterious allure. The very first eyelash curler, called Kurlash, was introduced in 1923 and was both complex and time-consuming, taking about ten minutes to work, and the most costly lashes, favored by the Hollywood legends, were made of seal, sable, mink, or human hair. In recent years, Shu Uemura has cornered the lash market creating the oft-lauded, astutely-designed curler in 1991, and adding different versions of false lashes to its repertoire every season since the '60s. And, as Dietrich would be pleased to discover, mink is still a favored material.

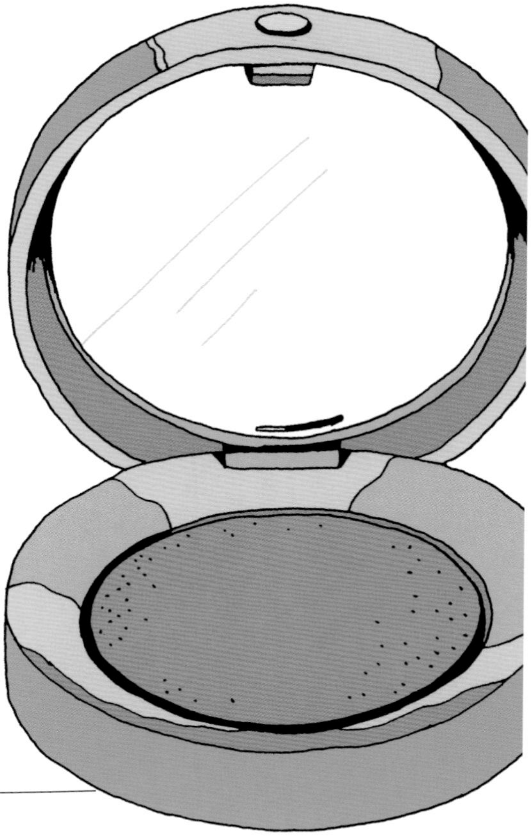

Little Round Pot Blush

It's interesting to learn that blush, seemingly the most girlish of all makeup products, was considered garish when worn by unmarried women in the States at the beginning of the twentieth century. But by the Roaring Twenties, our saucy Gallic neighbors had successfully wooed American women away from their cheek-pinching ways, thanks largely in part to Alexandre Napoleon Bourjois's dainty little round pots. In 1863, Bourjois invented his pièce de résistance—the first-ever dry-baked miniature pot of rouge spiked with a sweet Strawberry Shortcake-like scent. For years it was only manufactured in one shade, Cendre de Rose (Ashes of Rose), a brownish pink still available today. The classic little round pot now has a modern feel, seventeen more shades, and is available to both the loose and prudish woman.

Peace of Mind

peace of mind, n:
the absence of mental stress or anxiety

Origins has been true to its, er, origins since the very beginning. Conceived as a "natural beauty company" (the first of its kind), Origins sought to incorporate themes of wellness to create products that would make the consumer both look and feel good. And as environmental concerns have become increasingly paramount, the company's "green" approach to beauty has been welcomed into the cosmetics aisles. Origins' most iconic product was its very first: Peace of Mind On-the-Spot Relief. The tingly formula is designed to alleviate tension when you dab it on the base of your neck, temples, and earlobes. Eliminating the stresses of daily life—that's a trend that will never go out of style.

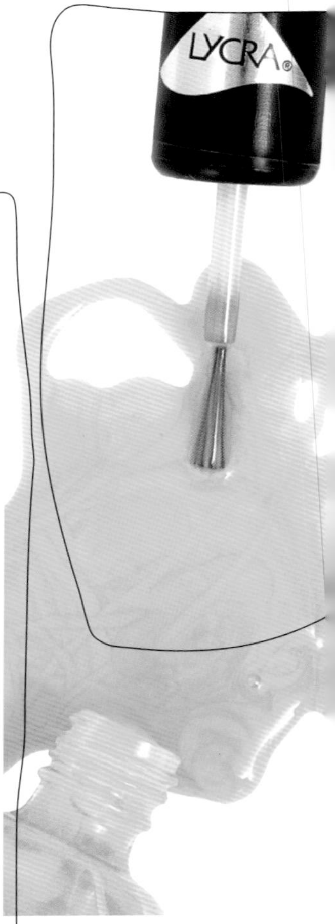

Lycra Wear Nail Polish

Lycra. The word alone is enough to elicit blood-curdling screams that can, in the worst cases, spiral into full-force panic attacks. You think fluorescent spandex bike shorts, gut-smashing girdles, and, gasp, bikinis! But there is one horror-free place on your body where Lycra can peacefully reside: your nails. The British brand Rimmel, famous for never turning its back on its very naughty cover girl Miss Moss, began infusing its nail polishes with the stretchy stuff in 2004. When added to enamel, Lycra has the same smoothing effect as in clothing, minimizing irregularities on the nail and increasing both shine and brilliance. The final product is a far cry from the brand's humbler polish offerings which first turned up on shelves in the '30s when nail painting became de rigueur.

Clean Makeup

Whether they were perched on a shelf in your locker or stuffed in your overflowing Caboodle, every child of the '80s remembers those little glass bottles of Cover Girl Clean foundation. They came in four shades of beige and were pretty much a required item for any self-respecting junior high school girl, along with stirrup pants and a crimping iron. But once you discover that the ingredients of said foundation are based almost entirely on another requisite pre-teen beautifier, Noxzema, you suddenly understand exactly why you were (and are still) obsessed. Turns out, when Cover Girl's parent company, P&G, bought Noxzema in the '50s, it created the groundbreaking foundation by simply adding flesh-toned pigments to its gentle formula. So it seems that the "good for your skin" tagline that has followed the product since its launch actually, well, fits.

LANCOME

Mascara

Perhaps it's the popular proverb "Eyes are the windows to the soul" that has prompted women over the years to use whatever means possible to draw attention to their peepers. Before mascara's invention, a 1905 issue of *Ladies Home Journal* advised women to apply India Ink to lashes so they might appear more noticeable. Once mascaras did hit shelves, consumers bought the crude formulas en masse so they might recreate the alluringly lengthy fringes that cloaked the peepers of Hollywood's most glamorous. In fact, when World War II created shortages that extended into the makeup market, women resorted to using boot wax as a temporary replacement. The '70s saw waterproof and a myriad of color versions, and in the '80s the catchword was "polymer," the revolutionary ingredient that boosted longevity. From Hypnose's customizable volume capabilities, to Flextencil's curving capacities, to, most recently, L'Extreme's knack for astounding lengthening, Lancôme is the undisputed leader in the prestige (aka not-available-in-drugstores) mascara category.

Pan-Cake Makeup

One of the very first Hollywood makeup artists and arguably the most influential, Max Factor, the son of Russian immigrants, was enamored of the stage and all of its trappings for his entire life. In the early days of film, way before Technicolor and radical retouching, actresses were thrust beneath the blaring lights wearing thick makeup that was spackled on their complexions in dull layers. Before Max Factor, that is. Realizing that the antiquated greasepaints left starlets looking flat and had a tendency to crack on film, Factor created Pan-Cake, a water-activated foundation that could, depending on how moist the application, be naturally sheer or flawlessly matte. And despite a very unfortunate name, the age-old formula is still prized today.

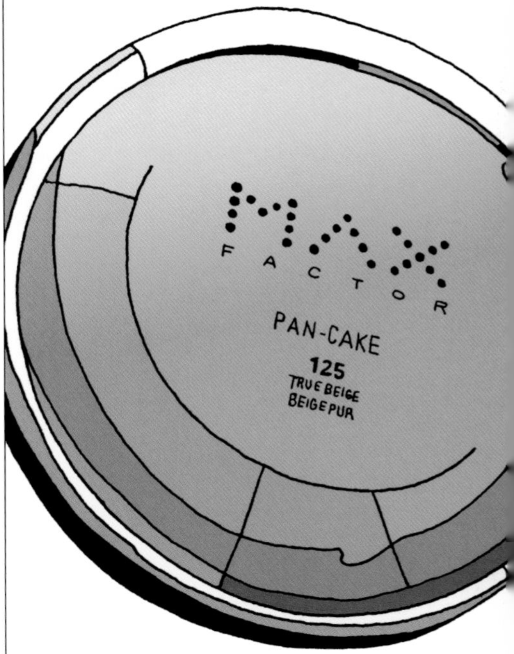

The Multiple

There was a time when women spent hours primping and preening in front of a mirror before placing themselves before the public eye. And while some "ladies who lunch" still consider the extra time they are able to spend beautifying a luxury, I can think of nothing more boring. Yes, I enjoy the process of transforming into a brassy Sally Bowles-era babe for a night out, but unless I suddenly switch careers (think Cabaret singer or, well, hooker), the idea of doing that every time I venture out of my house is exhausting. An everyday makeup routine should be simple. Enter François Nars, makeup genius and creator of the eponymous line of professional-quality cosmetics. NARS's 1996 innovation, the Multiple, a multipurpose cream-to-powder stick for eyes, lips, and cheeks in face-friendly shades, has quickly become an essential. Best of all, it requires zero fuss.

Terracotta

At the turn of the century, Victorian ideals of beauty—milky-white powdered skin, tiny lips, and doll-like ringlets—were firmly in place and widely accepted. Skin color remained the ultimate class marker—a tan, reddened visage was often acquired from time spent working in the fields, a profession reserved for the lower class. But this, like so many trends, changed with Coco Chanel. In 1920s France, only the most affluent, like Mademoiselle Chanel, could afford to travel on holiday to the luxurious beaches of Cannes and St. Tropez. Hence browned skin began to denote wealth, and companies like Jean Patou and L'Oréal quickly scrambled to create sun lotions to meet the growing demand. Alas, as was the case with so many other image-enhancing pleasures, the detrimental effect of sunbathing was eventually revealed, and the fear of skin cancer and premature aging sent many women scrambling for the shade. While the buzz of a cigarette can't be replicated, a tan most certainly can, and Guerlain revolutionized the bronzing category with the introduction of their Terracotta line in 1984, still a favorite among both consumers and makeup artists today.

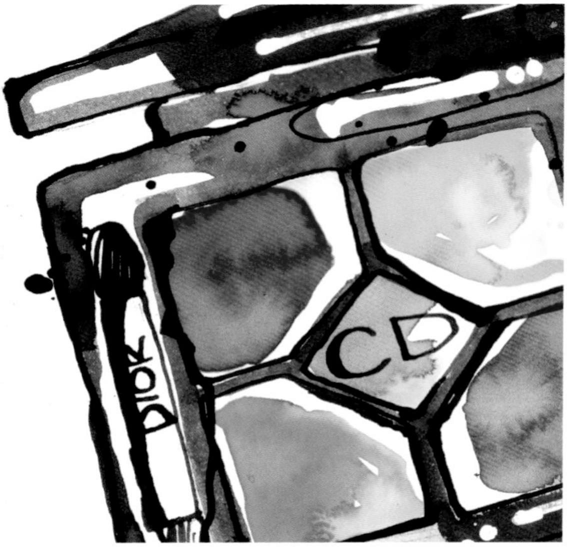

Miss Dior 5-Colour Shadows

At the turn of the century, before eye shadow became a commercial product, women desperate to add depth and definition to their eyes would reputedly mix Vaseline with newspaper ink to form a smoky paste for the lids. When shadows became widely available in the '20s, most were creamy, with hues either in brownish/black or turquoise/green. Within a decade, hundreds more shades were created, many infused with metallic undertones. Dior, whose beauty line has always been akin to fashion, is aware that versatility, when it comes to both makeup and clothing, is critical. Its signature five-shade shadow compacts allow for a wide range of styles, which, like the label's sartorial offerings, can be either flashy or modest.

CHANEL

Lipsticks

There is something undeniably provocative about watching a beautiful woman apply lipstick—the way the tube gently hovers between her fingertips and the fastidious attention paid to the pigment slowly being traced across her parted lips. Somewhere during the hullabaloo of the rollicking, Roaring Twenties, the act of putting on makeup in public went from vulgar to chic. Mademoiselle Coco Chanel, a woman who adored provocation of every sort, appreciated the power of a good red lipstick, so much so that it was the first product she developed for her cosmetics line. Coco was the originator of the ultra-androgynous *la garçonne* look popular at the time, which combined masculine tailoring with feminine makeup. That meant heavily coated lashes, cheeks painted with circles of rouge, and, of course, a ravishing red lip. No matter what the trend du jour, Chanel's lipsticks always fit the bill, from the very first Le 1er Rouge to the classic Rouge Hydrabase to the most recent Rouge Allure.

Lips & Tips

Charles Revson, the man behind Revlon, looked at nail polish as more than just a colored coating for your fingertips—to him it was a fashion accessory. And like fashion styles that change from season to season, so, thought Revson, should shades of nail enamel. After introducing the first creamy nail polish in the '30s, Revlon revolutionized the way women purchase cosmetics with its "Matching Lips and Fingertips" campaign that began in 1940. The ads read: "Pick up a tea-cup, light a cigarette, draw on a glove. Your slightest gesture delights the eye...with lips and fingertips accented vitally, fashionably by Revlon." Shade names like "Fifth Avenue Red" and "Cherries in the Snow" were chosen to evoke the same allure of elegance. Though for the majority of women (pageant participants aside) matching lips and nails is a dated concept, this will always remain a landmark idea in the history of cosmetic beauty.

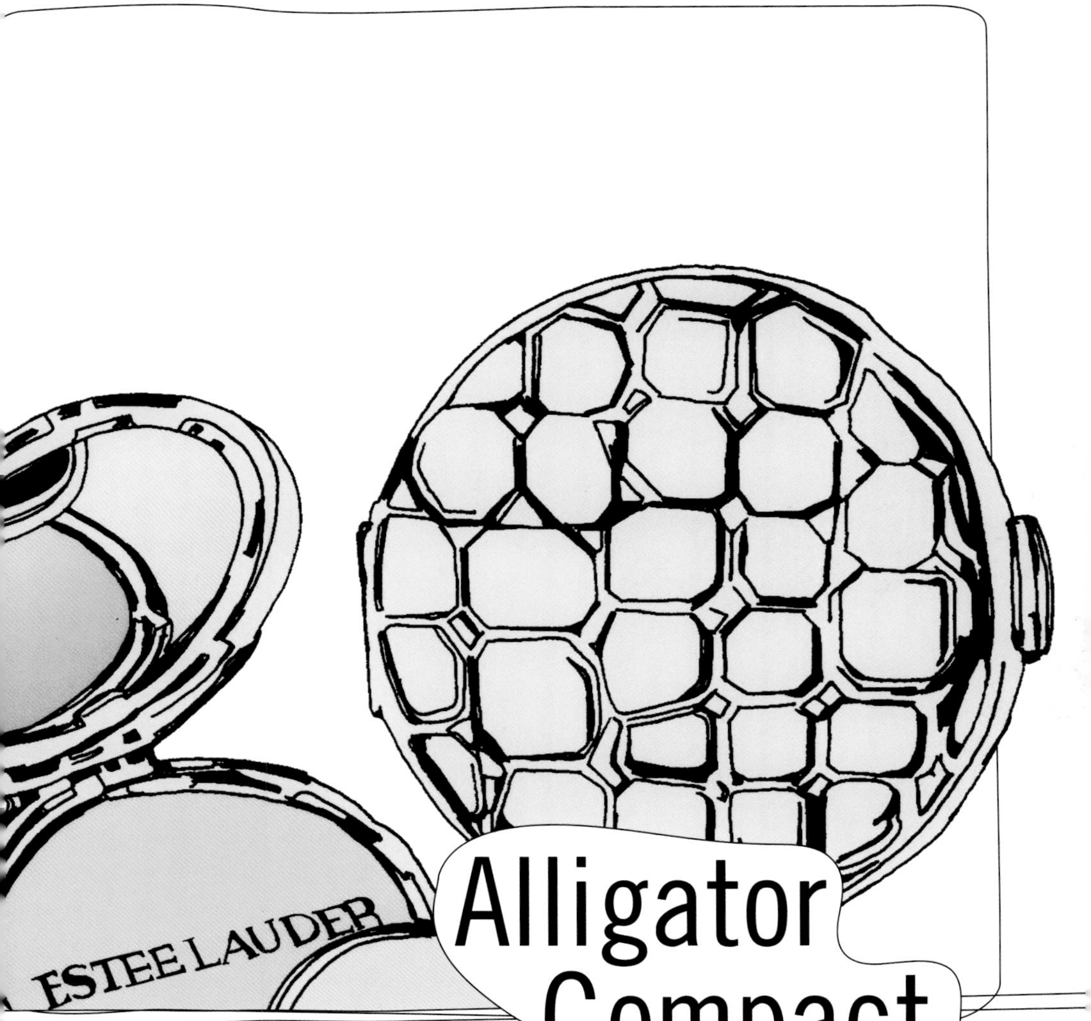

Alligator Compact

Everyone likes free. And often, it doesn't much matter what it is that you're getting, as long as it's gratis. Toothpick-speared bites of questionable origin become oddly appetizing when handed out at your local supermarket, and who could resist, despite the surefire heartburn that follows, the allure of the bottomless cup of coffee. But if free is what you're after, the department store beauty aisles are a veritable treasure trove. And Estée Lauder is whom you can thank—in 1946, the cosmetics giant became the very first to offer customers free samples. While the company's most iconic product, the luxurious golden pressed-powder compact that mirrors the alligator pattern of leather goods, is most certainly not free, you might feel more inclined to drop dough at a place that has long been so, ahem, generous.

Eudermine Lotion

The Japanese cosmetics company Shiseido made its debut in 1872 not with makeup, but with a skincare product. This decision, while initially considered odd, is in fact perfectly in tune with the company's mantra that the first step to a gorgeous face is luminous skin. And if there is one continent that I would have no qualms taking complexion counseling from, it is Asia—I challenge you to find an enlarged pore on Lucy Liu, or a blackhead on Ziyi Zhang. Eudermine's odd moniker comes from the Greek words "eu" meaning good, and "derma" meaning skin; it has been living up to its name since 1897. Eudermine is a transparent liquid that absorbs easily into the skin, smoothing and moisturizing the surface, accompanied by the scent of rain-soaked peonies. It's one import whose supply, we hope, is never restricted.

Great Lash

For as long as I can remember, Maybelline New York's iconic fluorescent pink-and-green-tubed mascara is the only trace of makeup my mom has ever used. As she likes to point out, in her youth she had a heavier hand when it came to cosmetics, but somewhere between kid one (me) and kid two (my brother), she lost both time and interest. But as streamlined as her routine, or lack thereof, became, "au naturel" always included two coats of Great Lash. The widely preferred drugstore mascara has been a hit since way back in 1915 when TL Williams founded Maybelline after watching his sister Mabel coat her lashes with petroleum jelly to make them more noticeable. Just like TL, I came to appreciate Great Lash's impact at a young age, and like so few other parental pointers, it's a lesson I actually retained.

Studio Fix

What do RuPaul, Pamela Anderson, and Lil' Kim have in common? Besides a shared penchant for gorgeous men, inflated breasts, and astonishingly high heels, they have all represented M.A.C cosmetics. And each one is a picture-perfect spokesmodel for a brand whose motto reads: "All ages, all races, all sexes, all M.A.C." If the beauty biz were a political hotbed, M.A.C would fall squarely on the far, far left, representing the interests of everyone from debutantes to drag queens to divas. Since the brand is firmly rooted in fashion, and has long had a pronounced presence during fashion weeks around the globe, it is no surprise that its star product is the one long favored by many a makeup artist: Studio Fix. The long-wearing powder foundation imparts a matte, velvety base for any skin tone, dark or light—the perfect canvas on which artists, novice or professional, can experiment.

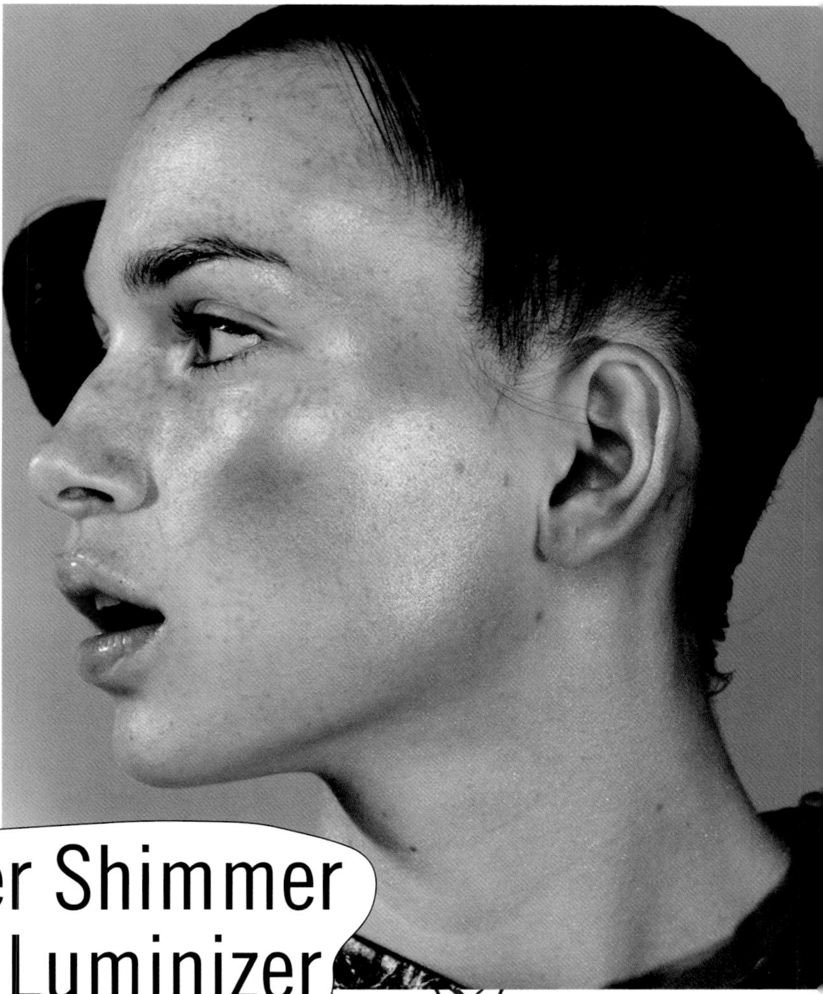

All Over Shimmer Liquid Luminizer

Make no mistake, there is a world of difference between glitter and shimmer. The former should be reserved for few things—children's art projects, Halloween costumes, and the Burning Man Festival—but the latter, when carefully incorporated into cosmetics, can be used without restraint. The integration of gold and silver shimmer into traditional shades of eye shadow first came about in the '30s, when many women sought to emulate the sheen of their favorite silver-screen stars. The '60s saw a deluge of golden glint as the sun-kissed boho look of women like Veruschka and Talitha Getty took hold, and the '90s heralded an all-out revival of all varieties of shimmer. And stila, the 1994 brainchild of celebrity makeup artist Jeanine Lobell, created the most versatile sparkly option in 2005. The brand's All Over Shimmer Liquid Luminizer is offered in white, pink, and gold, and can be applied on its own to lids, lips, cheeks, and collarbones, or mixed into your favorite foundation for an effect that is more luminous than gaudy.

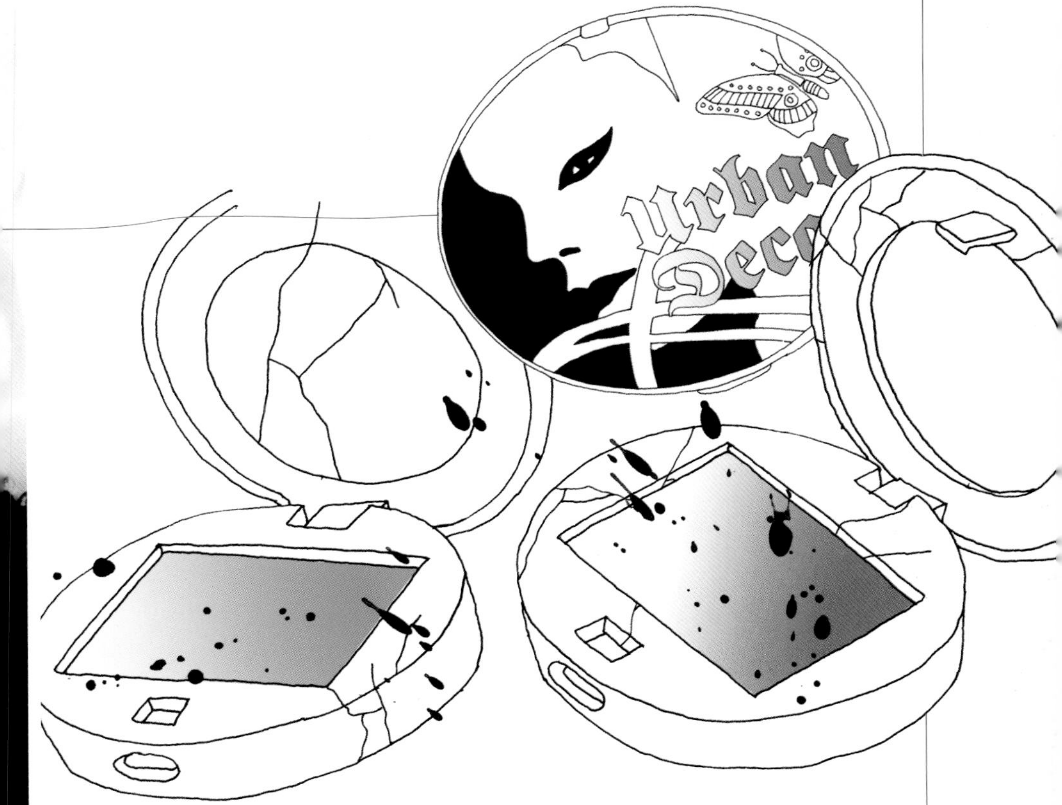

URBAN DECAY

Shadows

Uzi. Acid Rain. Asphyxia. Smog. Roach. Words not traditionally associated with cosmetics, until, that is, post-grunge era brand Urban Decay came along in 1996 inducting a street-wise edge into the beauty aisle. For Urban Decay, much of its allure was, to put it simply, in a name. The roughed-up monikers of all the products appealed to a very different audience than the company's clean-cut competitors—there is a virtual chasm between the teenage girl who gravitates toward Clinique and the ones who prefer Urban Decay. And the heavily pigmented shadows have remained the star product since the brand's inception, famous for their ability to incorporate shimmers, metallics, and micro-glitters to dramatic effect. Perfect for the rebel, young or old.

Touche Eclat

Anyone who has met a celebrity—especially one celebrated for her beauty—and been, well, disappointed understands immediately the importance of airbrushing and good lighting. (Anyone who has ever worked at a fashion magazine knows what we're talking about.) Well, consider Yves Saint Laurent your personal retoucher. His most genius of all makeup creations, Touche Eclat, does double duty as a magic wand and portable professional lighting team. The chic burnished pen-brush lightens any shadowy, under-eye circles and blends out the expression lines currently holding court around your mouth. It's silky, can be used under or over foundation and powder, and despite being produced in only three reflecting shades, imparts a perfect, just-had-sex-and-a-long-vacation glow to absolutely everyone.

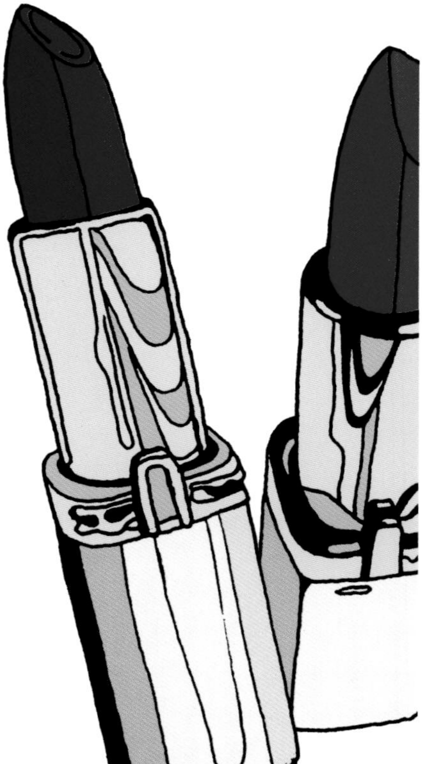

Colour Riche Lipstick

In the early part of the century, before Technicolor arrived in Hollywood, the lipstick coating the mouths of the most famous screen sirens had to be dark and dense enough to make an impression in black and white. It was a feat, which at the time required multiple coats and applications. But American women were so enamored of the painted pout that they were happy to reapply their favorite shades over and over again. In 1941, the *New York Times* reported that an astounding twenty million dollars worth of lipstick had been purchased that year. One has to wonder if the tube-count would have been as high if the formulas had been more advanced. When L'Oréal Colour Riche Lipstick was introduced in 1983 with rich, creamy, long-lasting colors like Mica, British Red Coat, and Brazil Nut, it instantly became an essential in every woman's cosmetic case because of both its durability and density.

Patrick Suskind's 1985 novel, *Perfume: The Story of a Murderer*, chronicled the obsession of one man who, though himself born without a personal odor, possessed a highly refined sense of smell, and was on a mission to create the perfect scent. It was an obsession which, as the title implies, had horrific consequences. While Suskind's was a fictional tale, it is, nonetheless, one that many relate to on some level. Scent is a sensation tightly intertwined with memory. We remember the scent of our grandmother's skin, a mélange of powdery perfume and baking flour. We remember the scent of the cheap cologne the boy who gave us our first kiss was drenched in. We remember the scents we each associate with childhood—the sugar-swathed fried dough at the local street fair; the clean, soapy No More Tangles shampoo; the rich trail of Old Spice that swirled off Dad's skin as he swung us above his shoulders; the heavy salt-cloaked air on our first trip to the ocean. If scent draws out memories, then perfume is a leading purveyor of nostalgia. Here are ten of the past century's most evocative fragrances.

HIGH

NOTES

N° 5
by Chanel

While the iconic image, most memorably immortalized by Warhol, may be more familiar than the aroma, it is Chanel N° 5's distinctive scent that has consistently secured it the status of best-selling perfume in the world since the '20s. In 1921, when Coco Chanel created N°5, in collaboration with legendary "nose" Ernest Beaux, she had very specific ideas in mind. "I want to give women an artificial fragrance," Chanel once claimed. "I say artificial because it will be fabricated. I want a fragrance that is composed…a women's fragrance that smells like women." And like her revolutionary clothing designs, she insisted that the perfume be unlike any other, with numerous contradictory facets. Beaux experimented with about eighty ingredients, mixing them into various aromatic concoctions for the five samples he presented to Chanel. She picked the fifth, insisting only that he add copious quantities of jasmine from the town of Grasse, perfume's most luxurious raw material.

Whether N°5 earned its moniker because it was the fifth of Beaux's samples, or simply because it had always been Mademoiselle's lucky number, is a continuing debate amongst perfume aficionados. Irregardless, the final fragrance was an inimitable mélange of notes like Comoro ylang-ylang, May rose, jasmine, sandalwood, and vanilla, housed in a simple, stamped bottle. N°5 was the first "abstract" composed fragrance, paving the way for a future generation of scents mixing natural and synthetic substances. And its inherent elegance was assured by the fact that only the world's most enticing stars—Ali McGraw, Lauren Hutton, Jean Shrimpton, Catherine Deneuve, Nicole Kidman—could serve as the face of the fragrance. But it was Marilyn who captured the spirit of Chanel best when, in 1954, a journalist famously asked the bombshell what she wore to bed, and she replied: "Just a few drops of N°5."

N°5
N°5
CHANEL
PARIS
PARFUM
N°5
CHANEL
PARIS
PARFUM

CHARLIE

by Revlon

The '70s were all about the Charlies: *Charlie's Angels*, Charles Manson, and Charlie by Revlon. Launched in 1973, and named after the founder of Revlon, Charles Revson, the inexpensive fragrance encapsulated a cultural moment and quickly became the number-one fragrance of the decade. It was the era of women's lib and Roe vs. Wade, and Revlon became the first company to forcefully market to a new "type" of woman. The scent itself—a floral combination of hyacinth, lily of the valley, and oakmoss—became almost a side note to the famous advertising campaign, which touted carefree, take-charge women who are in control of their lives, at home and in the workplace. The original ads created quite a buzz both in and out of the beauty industry because they were among the first to showcase women wearing pantsuits. They featured the perky jingle: "There's a fragrance that's here to stay and they call it...Charlie. Kinda fresh, kinda now, Charlie. Kinda new, kinda WOW, Charlie!" But there was one print advertisement that defined Charlie's ideals best—a picture of a businesswoman, briefcase in hand, laughing and playfully patting a man's behind with the slogan, "She's very Charlie." Indeed.

CK ONE by Calvin Klein

While nowadays the media frenzy around Kate Moss usually involves her reportedly rampant drug use and questionable choices in men, once upon a time the original waif was better known for inciting heated debates with her bony frame. The early '90s look was a rough-and-tumble combination of grunge and heroin chic, and thanks to Calvin Klein, Moss was its poster girl. In 1994, Klein, a designer famous for pushing the public's proverbial buttons with his racy campaigns (remember the preteen boys wearing underwear in wood-paneled basements?), summarized the edgy styles with the ad campaign for the first shared scent, ck One. Moss, along with Stella Tennant, Donovan Leitch and others, appeared in ck One's highly androgynous black-and-white advertisements photographed by Steven Meisel that would soon be pasted on billboards across the country. While the campaign was a pivotal moment in the world of advertising, it was the light, contemporary unisex scent of ck One itself, with notes of bergamot, cardamom, fresh pineapple, and musk, that would be even more groundbreaking.

Guerlain
Paris
SHALIMAR

YOUTH DEW

by Estée Lauder

"Time is not on your side, but I am." So quipped cosmetic entrepreneur Estée Lauder in her 1985 memoir, referring to her loyal customer base. That very philosophy was imbued in the array of products the company created, and, of course, in its first, defining fragrance, Youth Dew. Created in 1953, Youth Dew was in fact a perfumed bath oil formulated without an alcohol base, the first of its kind, which allowed the scent to linger longer on the skin. Lauder wisely began to market Youth Dew as a daytime perfume that women could use liberally rather than just dabbing conservatively behind the ears. It was a revelation during a time of French marketplace domination—85 percent of the perfume sold in the States in the late '40s was French. And Lauder would have to fight to have her economically priced perfume sold alongside its fancier counterparts—supposedly when one famous department store owner was reluctant about Youth Dew, Lauder "accidentally" broke a bottle on the floor and shoppers immediately became curious about the enthralling scent. A strong fragrance favored by strong women like Gloria Swanson and Joan Crawford, the spicy Bulgarian rose-laced concoction is still relevant today, re-interpreted most recently by the very able and oh-so-sexy hands of Tom Ford.

AROMATICS ELIXIR

by Clinique

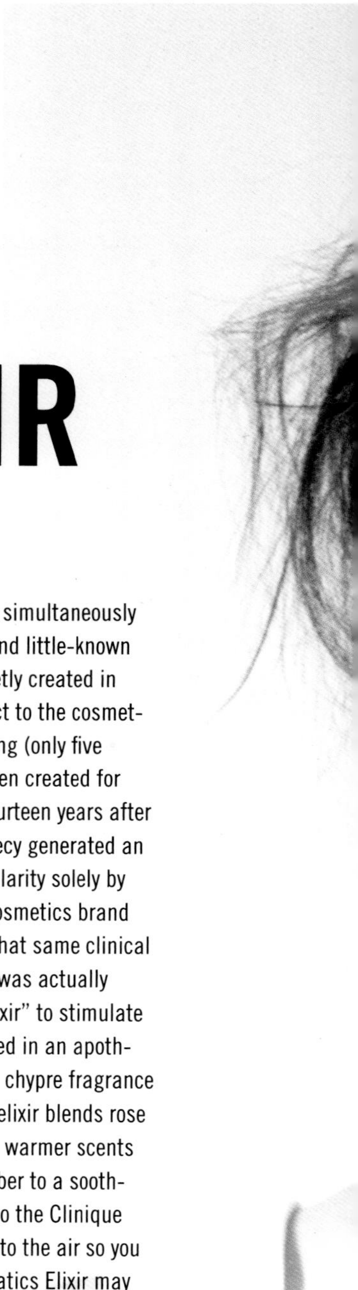

Clinique's Aromatics Elixir is simultaneously one of the most celebrated and little-known fragrances in the world. Quietly created in 1970 as a companion product to the cosmetics line, the lack of advertising (only five advertisements have ever been created for the perfume; the first was fourteen years after its launch) and general secrecy generated an immediate interest and popularity solely by word of mouth. Clinique, a cosmetics brand rooted in science, imparted that same clinical feel on the fragrance, which was actually classified as a "tonic" or "elixir" to stimulate the senses, and was presented in an apothecary-style bottle. Part of the chypre fragrance family, the mood-enhancing elixir blends rose essence and chamomile with warmer scents of patchouli, vetiver, and amber to a soothing finish, which, according to the Clinique experts, should be sprayed into the air so you can walk into the mist. Aromatics Elixir may still be considered a cult fragrance, but nowadays many more people are in the know—every minute, four bottles are snatched up by customers around the world.

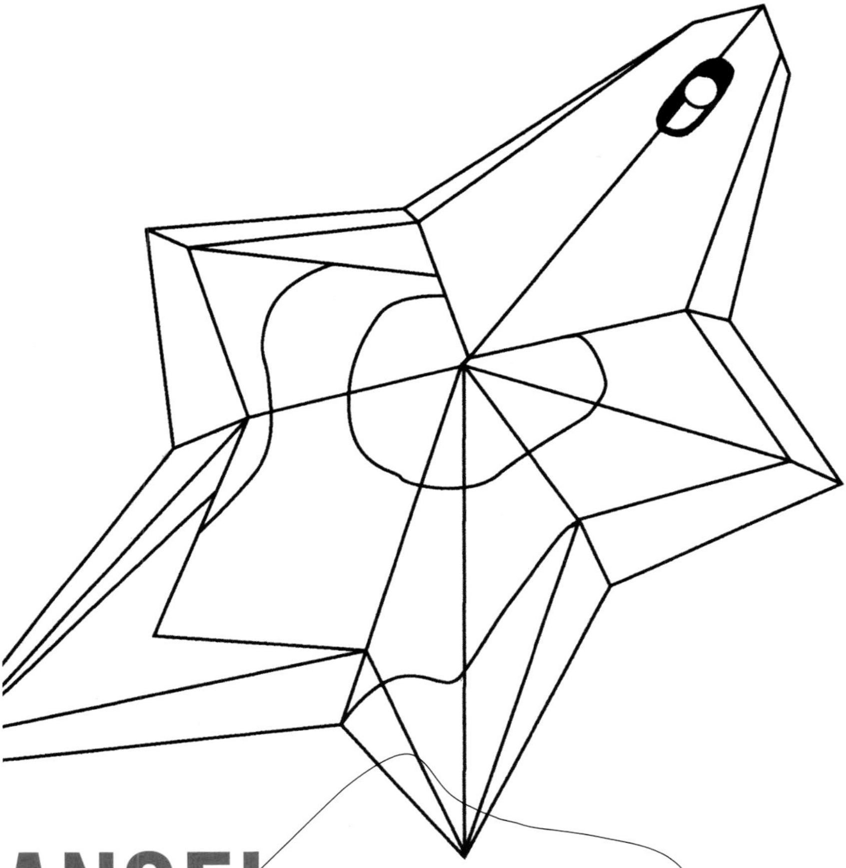

ANGEL by Thierry Mugler

For those with an insatiable sweet tooth, there is no more fitting fragrance than Angel, the original gourmand perfume created by Thierry Mugler in 1992. A sugary confection with a scent as mouthwatering as that of fresh-baked cookies, Angel was totally irresistible. "I always wanted to make a perfume which would have the same resonance for everyone," Mugler once said. "Something like tenderness, or childhood, and I wanted there to be such a sensual contact with this perfume, that you almost feel like devouring the person you love." Mugler's love of chocolate and his childhood memories of fair food (marshmallows, candy, and roasted almonds) were paired with perfumer Oliver Cresp's toasty vanilla and patchouli base. Even the star-shaped bottle—a shape inspired by Mugler's star obsession (he has one tattooed on his arm and another on a ring he always wears)—has a childlike whimsy about it. It is eternal youth, bottled.

OPIUM

by Yves Saint Laurent

If Bianca Jagger had been wearing a fragrance when she rode a white stallion into Studio 54 on the eve of her birthday in May 1977, during its drug-addled heyday, it would most certainly have been Yves Saint Laurent's irresistible Oriental, Opium. Created by Laurent in 1977 as a special fragrance for the Chinese empress, the scent heralded a return, amidst a sea of gentle florals, to the lavish Orientals popular at the beginning of the century. Even Opium's ornate flacon had Asian roots—the design was based on the inro, a tiny bottle which Far Eastern warriors clipped onto their belts to hold precious possessions. But Opium, because of its illicit name, would cause a sensation in circles far outside the fragrance industry. The perfume could only be released in the States after a federal investigation proved that the strong scent didn't promote drug use, and the original tagline, "For those who are addicted to Yves Saint Laurent," had to be amended to the less shocking, "For those who adore Yves Saint Laurent." Which model could represent such a scandalous scent? That honor went to Mrs. Mick Jagger number two, Texas troublemaker Jerry Hall.

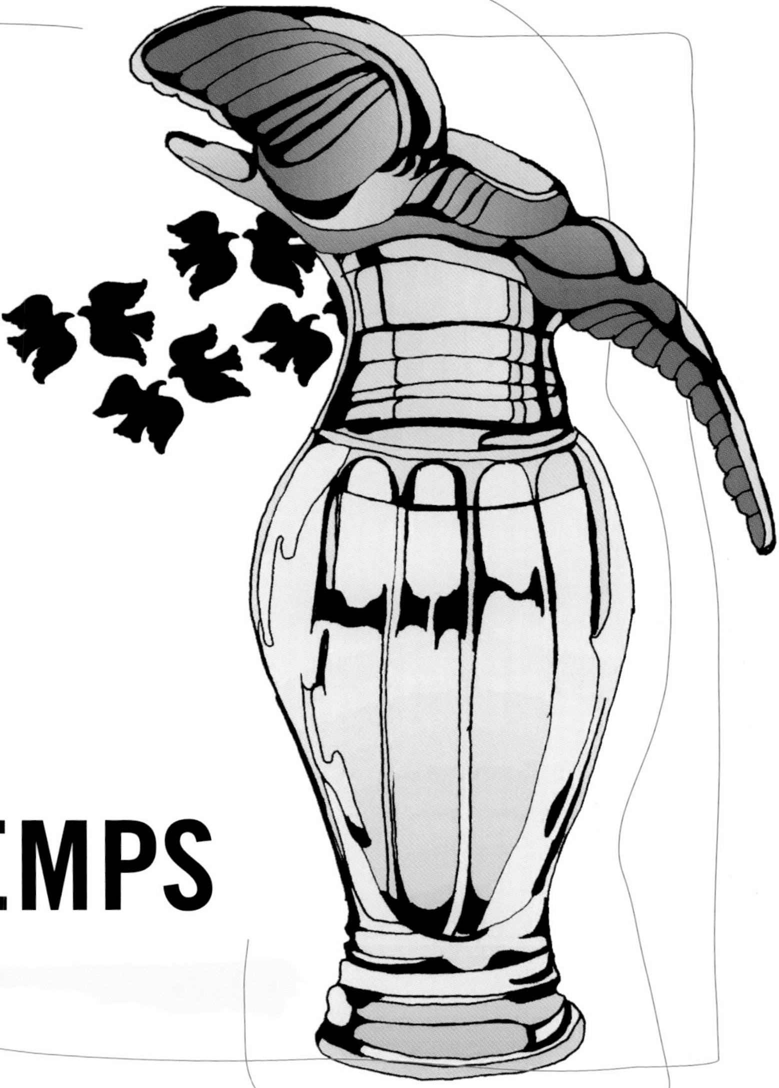

L'AIR DU TEMPS

by Nina Ricci

The French expression "l'air du temps" translates to "the mood of the moment." This sentiment was the inspiration behind French couturier Nina Ricci's first fragrance, which bears that name. The troubled years around World War II saw a decline in both the fragrance and cosmetics industries, and a general step back from the luxuries of decades past. With the release of L'Air du Temps in 1948, Robert Ricci (Nina's son) sought to create a simple, beautiful perfume that was a celebration of both love and peace, and that was, above all, resolutely feminine. He was the first perfumer to utilize benzyl salicylate, a new synthetic product which gave the fragrance a blooming effect on the skin. But it wasn't simply the powdery floral carnation/gardenia blend that made L'Air du Temps momentous, it was the ornate presentation. The graceful Lalique-designed bottle was topped with two doves in flight, the classic symbol of peace, and came nestled in a white-and-yellow silk-lined box. L'Air du Temps would become the grandmother of many future florals and also serve as an inspiration for legions of over-the-top bottle designs.

FRACAS

by Robert Piguet

There are mega-companies that easily produce fragrance after fragrance, each with its corresponding reception by massive audiences. And then there are the "indie" houses that create only a handful of perfumes to the accolades of a much smaller, but no less appreciative audience. Robert Piguet fell comfortably into the latter category. The couturier's name was on people's tongues in Paris in the '30s and '40s but, unlike Chanel, for instance, Piguet's greatest success came not as a designer, but as a teacher and mentor to future generations (Pierre Balmain, Hubert de Givenchy, and Christian Dior were all pupils), and as the man behind one of the most infamous cult fragrances of all time, Fracas. The reserved elegance of Piguet's typically *parisien* clothing style was translated into a perfume that was both simple and sumptuous. An overwhelmingly creamy tuberose is melded with a bouquet of white flowers like gardenia, jasmine, and lily of the valley and a sandalwood base to create an alarmingly seductive scent sexy enough to be favored by the ultimate provocateur herself, Madonna.

fracas
DE
ROBERT
PIGUET
PARIS-FRANCE

PART

2 THE INSPIRATION

PRIVATE

Each decade has them—the head turners, the pinups, the idols, the leading ladies, the trendsetters, the sex symbols. They are the stylistic rabble-rousers, and at *NYLON*, they are crowned each month as our Private Icons. Beyond its religious symbolism, an icon is defined as "someone who is the object of great attention and devotion." These breathtaking women (and men), culled from the worlds of film, music, television, and various other media and separated into the decades in which their influence was strongest, all fit the bill. But while every chosen woman's (or man's) personal style inspired countless others at the peak of his or her fame, it is each one's ability to maintain that notoriety and cultural cachet years beyond his or her proverbial prime that makes them icons. Let the reverence begin.

CONS

1920s &'30s

What qualified as attractive during the rollicking '20s and '30s was the antithesis of natural beauty—the allure was in the artificial. The '20s saw brows plucked and sharply sketched to anorexic silhouettes, cheeks painted with doll-like spheres of rouge, lashes layered with mascara, lips drawn in bow-tie form, and hair cropped and waved. While the '30s face remained obviously painted, it was less exaggerated. The desired look—feathery false lashes and dark, precisely applied lipstick—came courtesy of Hollywood, and women like Marlene Dietrich and Joan Crawford. Women's laborious hair and makeup efforts throughout this period were evident, and that's just the way they liked it.

GINGER ROGERS

M.A.C LONGWEAR LIPCOLOUR IN COMMITMENT
ROGERS NEEDED A LIPSTICK THAT WOULD STAY PUT THROUGH HER LONG DANCE SEQUENCES.

ORIGINS GINGER WITH A TWIST MOISTURIZING BODY COOLER
A SCENT AS SWEET AS THE SCREEN STAR.

DOVE DEEP MOISTURE FACIAL LOTION
THE PERFECT PRODUCT FOR FRESH-FACED AMERICAN GIRL

Ginger Rogers's first foray into show business was as part of a traveling vaudeville act alongside her mom, Lela. It was while on tour that the teenage, cherubic-looking blonde met Jack Pepper, a fellow performer who would become the first of her five husbands. Thankfully, she had more staying power in her professional life. After moving to New York to work in theater, Rogers made a mark in productions like Gershwin's *Girl Crazy*, and soon was on her way to the West Coast, where her knack for singing and dancing would prove handy in films like *Gold Diggers of 1933*, which featured the now-famous tune "The Gold Diggers' Song (We're in the Money)." But what really launched Rogers's career was her charismatic on-screen partnership with Fred Astaire. They made ten musicals together, including *Top Hat* (1935) and *Swing Time* (1936), that were box-office hits not only because of the duo's chemistry, but because the glamorous settings proved a welcome escape for moviegoers during the Depression. Rogers, a devout Christian Scientist and longtime conservative Republican, never smoked or drank and was far removed from much of Hollywood's shenanigans. When asked of the pairing that made her famous, Rogers once said, "We had fun and it shows. True, we were never bosom buddies off the screen; we were different people with different interests. We were only a couple on film."

LILLIAN GISH

Lillian Gish was known as "the first lady of the silent screen," and was a force to be reckoned with at the turn of the century. Though she had been acting since her youth, it was only after her friend Mary Pickford introduced her to the director D.W. Griffith that she began to land plum roles. The tiny, fragile-featured actress emoted easily on the silent screen, delivering impressive performances in *The Birth of a Nation* (1915) and *Intolerance* (1916). And while many actors were constrained before the addition of sound, Gish found a real grace without it. "I never approved of talkies," she claimed. "Silent movies were well on their way to developing an entirely new art form. It was not just pantomime, but something wonderfully expressive." Gish would showcase her silent-screen abilities in a few more movies like *The Scarlet Letter* (1926) and *The Wind* (1928) before taking a break from Hollywood to focus on the stage. But she was never forgotten—the Smashing Pumpkins even named their 1994 album *Gish* after her.

DIVINE MOISTURIZING CLEANSING CREAM
WHETHER IN COLOR OR IN BLACK AND WHITE, RADIANT SKIN WILL ALWAYS SHINE ON SCREEN.

BÉSAME BOUDOIR ROUGE IN SWEET PINK
THE WOMEN OF THIS ERA LOVED THEIR ROUGE AND WOULD APPLY IT IN ROUND CIRCLES.

THIERRY MUGLER INNOCENT EAU DE PARFUM
GISH LOOKED INNOCENT ENOUGH TO BE A CHILD WELL INTO MIDDLE AGE.

GRETA GARBO

It was luck that won Greta Garbo, a working-class Swedish girl, a scholarship to Stockholm's prestigious Royal Dramatic Theatre, where she was discovered by director Mauritz Stiller. Though Stiller would propel Garbo's Hollywood career, the statuesque Swede wowed audiences all on her own from the moment she first appeared on film. It was on the set of the landmark silent movies *Flesh and the Devil* (1926) and *Love* (1927) that she met actor John Gilbert with whom she had a highly publicized romance (and whom she eventually abandoned at the altar). Garbo seamlessly made the transition to "talkies" with 1931's *Anna Christie* (advertised with the slogan "Garbo Talks!"), likely because her husky, accented voice added to her mysterious allure. The famous line from *Grand Hotel* (1932), "I want to be left alone," would become her mantra—after Gilbert, Garbo kept her personal life personal, despite waves of media speculation. She purportedly had a number of lesbian lovers including Louise Brooks, Claudette Colbert, Marlene Dietrich, and the writer Mercedes de Acosta. But despite earning numerous accolades and four Oscar nominations for her acting, Garbo retreated from Hollywood and spent much of her later years as a recluse.

CHANEL
ALLURE
high performance balancing cleansing oil since 1960
SHU UEMURA SKIN PURIFIER
julie hewett
los angeles

ALLURE BY CHANEL
NOT THAT GARBO NEEDED MUCH HELP IN THE ALLURE DEPARTMENT.

JULIE HEWETT HUE COLOUR IN NEWSPRINT BLEU
AFTER GARBO'S MOVIE DEBUT, A COLUMNIST WROTE, "UNTIL THE APPEARANCE OF THOSE LUSCIOUS GARBO CLOSE-UPS, HEAVY-LIDDED AND LANGUOROUS, OUR GIRLS NEVER PAID GREAT ATTENTION TO THEIR EYES... NOW EVEN OUR NICEST PEOPLE HAVE BEGUN TO USE MASCARA AND EYE SHADOW."

SHU UEMURA CLEANSING OIL SKIN PURIFIER
ONLY THE BEST WOULD SUFFICE FOR A WOMAN WHO EARNED THE NICKNAMES "THE FACE" AND "THE SPHINX" BECAUSE OF HER STUNNING VISAGE.

L'ORÉAL HIP LIPCOLOUR IN VIVACIOUS 558
"I'VE LIVED BY A MAN'S CODE DESIGNED TO FIT A MAN'S WORLD, YET AT THE SAME TIME I NEVER FORGET THAT A WOMAN'S FIRST JOB IS TO CHOOSE THE RIGHT SHADE OF LIPSTICK."

GOSMILE DAILY COMPACT
WHEN YOU LAUGH FOR A LIVING, WHITE TEETH ARE ESSENTIAL.

KIEHL'S MALLEABLE MOLDING PASTE
HER SHORT, WAVY BOB WAS ALWAYS SMOOTH AND SLEEK.

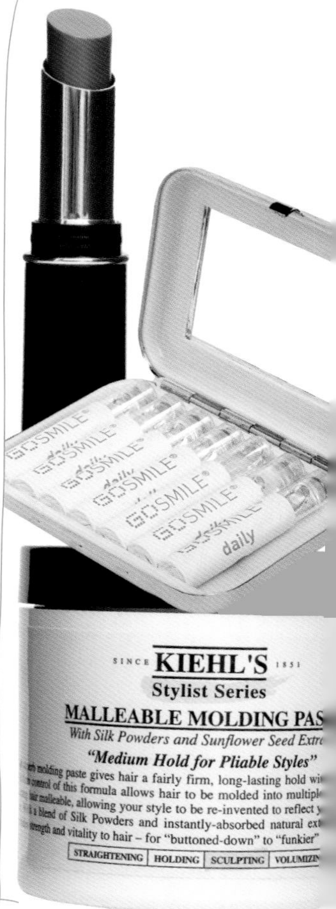

CAROLE LOMBARD

Carole Lombard was discovered at age twelve while playing baseball on the street with her brothers, and quickly cast in 1921's *A Perfect Crime*, but she would wait until her mid-teens before dropping out of school to pursue acting full time. Lombard, an icy blonde with a beaming smile, quickly became "the queen of screwball comedy" in the '30s. Her appearance may have been sophisticated, but Lombard was unafraid to look like a fool on-screen for the sake of a joke—she and John Barrymore hammed it up in *Twentieth Century* (1934), and she pulled in an Oscar nod for her turn as a dizzy socialite opposite her ex-husband William Powell in *My Man Godfrey* (1936). Besides getting laughs on screen, Lombard was also famous for her practical jokes and potty mouth off set, earning her the nickname "the profane angel." Perhaps it was those dirty jokes that lured in her oh-so-dashing husband Clark Gable—the two met on the set of *No Man of Her Own* (1932) and were married in 1939. Sadly, Lombard's life and career were cut far too short—she, her mom, and twenty others were killed in a plane crash in 1942 while returning from a war bonds campaign.

DOLORES DEL RIO

CAROLINA HERRERA FRAGRANCE
FROM ONE FAMOUS SENORITA TO ANOTHER.

LOLA GLO-LA SHIMMERING BODY OIL IN BRONZED GODDESS
HER NICKNAME WAS LOLITA SO SHE WOULD HAVE BEEN ENAMORED OF THIS LINE.

DARPHIN HYDRASKIN NIGHT CREAM
DEL RIO REPORTEDLY SLEPT SIXTEEN HOURS A DAY TO MAINTAIN HER BEAUTY.

Born in Durango, Mexico, Dolores del Rio was the first major Mexican movie star. She was picked at twenty-one as one of WAMPAS' (Western Association of Motion Picture Advertisers) "baby stars" of 1926—an honor given in the '20s to thirteen young women per year who were believed to be headed for stardom—along with Joan Crawford and Fay Wray. Del Rio first caught the public's eyes in the 1926 silent film *What Price Glory?* Though she was often confined, because of her accent, to the role of exotic foreigner, del Rio made no less of an impression in films such as *Bird of Paradise* (1932), *Flying Down to Rio* (1933), and *Madame DuBarry* (1934). But while she longed to be taken seriously for her acting, her stunning beauty was hard to ignore. Del Rio was petite and curvaceous with ebony-colored hair and dark, mysterious eyes. After her divorce from MGM art director Cedric Gibbons in 1941, she was pursued by a slew of male suitors, including Orson Welles.

CLARA BOW

L'OCCITANE ROSE VELVET BODY CREAM
AS THE SONG GOES, EVERY ROSE HAS ITS THORN... BOW HAD A FEW.

MAX FACTOR COLOUR PERFECTION LIPSTICK IN BORDEAUX
IT WAS FACTOR WHO WAS RESPONSIBLE FOR CREATING BOW'S FAMOUS BOW-TIE LIPS.

GUERLAIN NAIL ENAMEL IN ROUGE HOLLYWOOD
THE FIRST POLISHES WERE INTRODUCED IN 1925 AND WERE OFTEN APPLIED ONLY TO THE MIDDLE OF THE NAIL, LEAVING THE TIP BARE.

Pre-Kirsten, pre-Maggie, pre-Scarlett, there was the original "It Girl"—the one for whom the term was actually coined. Clara Bow, the darling of the Roaring Twenties silent films, was bestowed with the now-famous title (or epithet, depending on your point of view) after starring, fittingly enough, in *It* (1927), as a shopgirl seduced by her boss. Often described in the press as "flaming youth in rebellion," the petite actress continued to find fame in a number of movies by playing the working girl who challenged Victorian mores, a fact her legions of fans (she reportedly received 45,000 letters a week at the height of her career) appreciated. But it wasn't just on-screen that Bow courted scandal: her coarse public persona (and numerous affairs) made her something of a pariah in celebrity circles. Born in 1905 in Brooklyn to a schizophrenic mom and an abusive dad, Bow made her way to Hollywood after winning a local beauty pageant. Though silent films were very good to her, once sound entered the picture, her heavy New York accent held her back. Eventually, the sad-eyed star with the signature ringlets and drawn-on brows followed in her mother's footsteps, succumbing to mental illness.

KÉRASTASE NUTRITIVE BAIN ELASTRO-CURL CONDITIONER
HER BLONDE CURLS GAVE HER A DOLL-LIKE APPEARANCE.

PRESCRIPTIVES LASH ENVY VOLUMIZING MASCARA
DAVIES PROVED THAT CLUMPY LASHES ARE NOT ALWAYS A BEAUTY FAUX PAS.

BY TERRY ROUGE DELECTATION IN PLUM MARMALADE
PERHAPS IT WAS HER PERFECTLY PAINTED POUT THAT LURED IN CHARLIE CHAPLIN, WITH WHOM SHE REPUTEDLY HAD AN AFFAIR.

MARION DAVIES

Born and raised in Brooklyn, Marion Cecelia Douras (she and her sisters changed their last name to Davies after seeing it on a neighborhood realtor's sign) first gained notoriety as one of the chorus girls in the *Ziegfeld Follies*. But dancing didn't interest this curly-haired blonde—she wanted to act. Davies went on to appear in a string of silent films like *The Cinema Murder* (1919) and *When Knighthood Was in Flower* (1922), but, despite her trepidation due to a childhood stutter, she really shined as a comedic actress in '30s talking films like *The Florodora Girl* (1930) and *Not So Dumb* (1930). But Davies was also recognized then and remembered now for her tumultuous long-term affair with billionaire media mogul William Randolph Hearst. They lived together in the infamous San Simeon mansion, the site of lavish parties and the mysterious murder of Thomas Ince, chronicled in 2001's *The Cat's Meow*, in which Kirsten Dunst played Davies.

JERGENS SOFT SHIMMER MOISTURIZER
WITH THAT MUCH SKIN EXPOSED, BAKER COULD HAVE USED SOMETHING TO KEEP IT SHINY AND GLOWING.

DAVINES WIZARDS GLOSSY MODELING PUTTY
BAKER'S CLOSELY CROPPED HAIR WAS ALWAYS SHINY.

GUERLAIN TERRACOTTA LOOSE POWDER KOHL LINER IN BLACK 1
BAKER LOVED TO OUTLINE HER EYES IN DARK KOHL TO ADD AN AIR OF DRAMA.

JOSEPHINE BAKER

The African-American dancer, singer, and sometime actress may have been born in the States, but France, where she became a citizen in 1937, was her true home. Though she was popular in New York during the Harlem Renaissance, it was when she moved to Paris to join La Revue Nègre that her career really took off. Her erotically charged, nearly nude performances led to her most famous turn at the Folies Bergères. There she danced for capacity crowds wearing not much more than a bunch of bananas strung into a skirt and accompanied by her leopard named Chiquita. Baker was one of the most photographed women of her time, a muse for a number of artists, including Pablo Picasso, and a superstar amongst her fans who showered her with gifts and marriage proposals (she was rumored to have received more than 1,500 over the years). Hemingway once described her as "the most sensational woman anyone ever saw." Offstage, Baker was just as fascinating—she married and divorced four (or more) times, worked as a spy for the French Resistance during World War II, refused to play in racially segregated clubs, and eventually adopted twelve children from around the world to form what she deemed "The Rainbow Tribe."

BETTE DAVIS

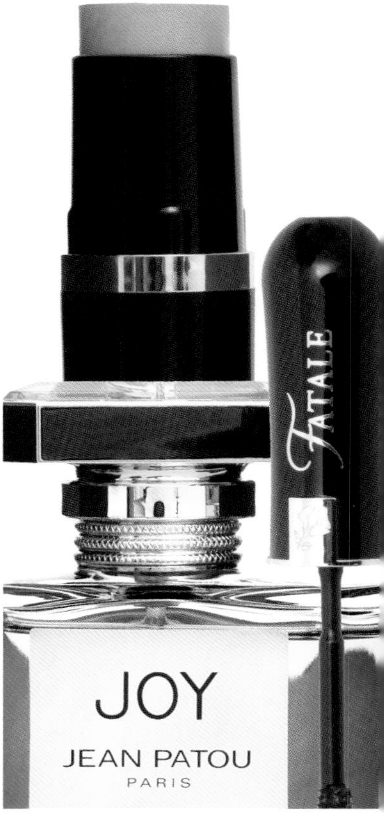

MAX FACTOR PAN-STIK FOUNDATION FACTOR'S TRANSPARENT, MATTE FOUNDATION WAS A MIRACLE WORKER ON FILM SETS.

JOY BY JEAN PATOU ONLY DAVIS COULD PULL OFF A HEAVY, INTOXICATING PERFUME LIKE JOY, AND BOTH STAR AND SCENT WERE INTRODUCED IN 1931.

LANCÔME FATALE MASCARA EYES THIS LEGENDA —THEY EVENTUALLY INSPIRED KIM CARNE HIT SONG—NEED A GOOD MASCARA.

Besides being one of the most celebrated actresses of the last century, Bette Davis was also one of the most brazen—if Harlow was the original blonde bombshell, Davis was the original diva. Born in Lowell, Massachusetts, Davis elbowed her way to Hollywood, quickly establishing herself as a force to be reckoned with, and picking up nicknames like "the Fifth Warner Brother" along the way. Davis always played strong, significant characters, and earned critical acclaim for her roles in movies like *Of Human Bondage* (1934), *Dangerous* (1935), and *Jezebel* (1938). But while her performances on-screen were memorable—she won Oscars for her roles in *Dangerous* and *Jezebel*—she'll go down in history for her droll, sarcastic remarks on everything from her co-stars ("I wouldn't piss on her if she was on fire," referring to Joan Crawford) to aging ("Getting old is not for sissies") to Hollywood ("Until you're known in my profession as a monster, you're not a star") to marriage ("I'd marry again if I found a man who had fifteen million dollars, would sign over half to me, and guarantee that he'd be dead within a year"). Her pit-bull determination opened up doors for women—she was the president of the Academy of Motion Picture Arts and Sciences and was the first actress awarded the Lifetime Achievement Award by the AFI. She continued to act into the '50s and beyond, garnering particular acclaim for her roles in *All About Eve* (1950) and *What Ever Happened to Baby Jane?* (1962)—alongside her nemesis Joan Crawford.

MARLENE DIETRICH
in *The Blue Angel*

Marlene Dietrich was a femme fatale on and off the screen. She appeared in a string of German silent films before landing Europe's first "talkie," Josef von Sternberg's *The Blue Angel* (1930) as the leggy, lust-filled Lola Lola, a seductive nightclub singer who drives a local teacher into a tizzy. Lola's throaty rendition of "Falling in Love Again," while wearing not much more than a top hat and stockings, was easily the decade's sexiest performance—it would make young Dietrich a star and reveal the husky voice that would become her trademark. Von Sternberg, with whom she was carrying on an affair, brought the German actress to Hollywood, where she was often cast as the gorgeous girl of questionable moral standing in such movies as *Morocco* (1930), *Shanghai Express* (1932), and *Blonde Venus* (1932).

L'ORÉAL ENDLESS KISSABLE LIPCOLOUR IN RUBY RUBY
ONE OF HER MAKEUP ARTISTS ONCE CLAIMED THAT DIETRICH KISSED SO HARD THAT SHE NEEDED A NEW COAT OF LIPSTICK AFTER EACH SMOOCH.

MAYBELLINE NEW YORK EXPERT EYES TWIN BROW AND EYE PENCILS IN CHARCOAL GREY
WHAT BETTER MATCH FOR THOSE SEDUCTIVE BEDROOM EYES THAN A SEVERE DRAWN-IN BROW?

BUMBLE AND BUMBLE BB HAIR SHINE
SHE REPORTEDLY ONCE ASKED MAX FACTOR TO SPRINKLE AN OUNCE OF GOLD DUST INTO HER WIGS.

Her personal life was just as incendiary—Dietrich had a string of male (including three members of the Kennedy clan) and female lovers (including Mae West, Joan Crawford, Greta Garbo, and Claudette Colbert), and once famously quipped: "In Europe it doesn't matter if you're a man or a woman—we make love with anyone we find attractive." The often-androgynous Dietrich became such a hit in Hollywood that her native Germany begged her to return, but because of her stalwart anti-Nazi stance, she refused and supported her adopted country's USO efforts instead.

JOAN CRAWFORD

Despite a childhood foot injury, this actress began her illustrious career as a chorus dancer in New York under her given name, Lucille LeSueur. After she signed with MGM, studio execs thought her last name sounded a bit too much like "sewer"—it was a reader contest in a popular movie magazine that bestowed upon the budding actress her new moniker, Joan Crawford. Crawford became a regular on the silver screen in the '20s and '30s, most often playing the sassy, independent woman in rags to riches tales—a factory worker in *Possessed* (1931), a secretary in *Grand Hotel* (1932), a shopgirl in *The Women* (1939). Married five times and allegedly bisexual (she was linked to Barbara Stanwyck and Marilyn Monroe), Crawford had a love of all things dramatic that extended far beyond the movie set, with her personal life often becoming public fodder. In her later years, much of the drama was focused on her child-rearing abilities, particularly after her daughter Christina penned the exposé *Mommie Dearest*, which was made into a film after the actress's death. Though Crawford dropped in and out of Hollywood—one comeback as Bette Davis's terrorized sister in 1962's *What Ever Happened to Baby Jane?* is unforgettable—she always looked like a somebody. Crawford once quipped, "I never go out unless I look like Joan Crawford the movie star. If you want to see the girl next door, go next door."

DERMALOGICA DAILY MICROFOLIANT
CRAWFORD ONCE CLAIMED, "I NEED SEX FOR A CLEAR COMPLEXION, BUT I'D RATHER DO IT FOR LOVE." PERHAPS A PURIFYING CLEANSER LIKE THIS WOULD HAVE HELPED.

MAX FACTOR COLOUR PERFECTION LIPSTICK IN CHIANTI
WHEN CRAWFORD GREW TIRED OF HER THIN LIPS, MAKEUP ARTIST MAX FACTOR ARTFULLY SMEARED LIPSTICK ACROSS HER UPPER AND LOWER LIPS. THE SMEAR OR "HUNTER'S BOW" WOULD BECOME A SIGNATURE LOOK.

AWAKE COSMETICS STARDOM POWDER IN VENUS SEA
SHE WAS A STAR IN EVERY SENSE, AND SHE ALWAYS WANTED TO LOOK THE PART.

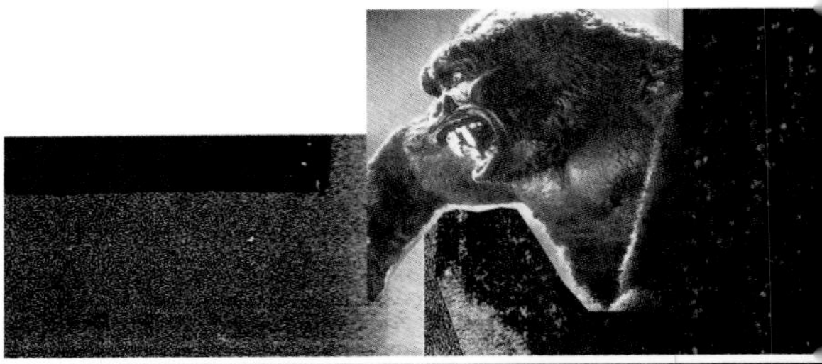

MAYBELLINE NEW YORK SUPERSTAY LIPCOLOR IN RASPBERRY
WITH SO MUCH ATTENTION ON HER MOUTH, WRAY NEEDED A RELIABLE LIPSTICK.

DR. BRANDT DAILY UV PROTECTION SPF 30
THE FILM WAS SET IN A TROPICAL LOCATION, SO WRAY NEEDED TO PROTECT HER PALE SKIN FROM THE SUN WHILE IN KONG'S CLUTCHES.

VERY IRRESISTIBLE BY GIVENCHY
THOUGH THE APE DIDN'T NEED MUCH IMPETUS, THIS DESIR- ABLE SCENT WOULD HAVE REALLY DRIVEN HIM WILD.

FAY WRAY in *KING KONG*

How did a movie about the relationship between a gorgeous washed-up actress and an ape become a symbol of Hollywood-made fantasy that endures today? Perhaps it was the "beauty and the beast" element that had such sweeping appeal, or maybe the simple glorious campiness of it all, but whatever the factor, 1933's *King Kong* became a legend, and made a Hollywood star out of the Canadian-born Fay Wray. Though she had been acting since her teens in low-budget films, and offered up a stellar performance as the innkeeper's daughter, Mitzi Schrammell, in *The Wedding March* (1928), it was *King Kong* that Wray will always be remembered for. Ann Darrow, a role for which Wray donned a blonde wig, earned her the title of "The Queen of Scream" for the glass-shattering shrieks she needed to deliver at top volume when in the hands of the beast. Wray once said, "At the premiere of *King Kong*, I wasn't too impressed. I thought there was too much screaming...I didn't realize then that *King Kong* and I were going to be together for the rest of our lives." Despite her best efforts to seek out more serious roles, her screaming prowess landed her roles in a number of other B-horror movies. But the legend endures—Naomi Watts filled her shoes in Peter Jackson's 2005 remake of the horror classic.

PHILOSOPHY BABY GRACE SPRAY FRAGRANCE
HER FRIENDS KNEW HER AS "BABY"—EVEN HER TOMBSTONE IS INSCRIBED WITH THE WORDS "OUR BABY."

CLAIROL HERBAL ESSENCES SHEER DIAMOND EXTRA LIGHT COOL BLONDE
AFTER APPEARING IN *HELL'S ANGELS*, HARLOW STARTED A NATIONWIDE CRAZE FOR BLEACHED BLONDE HAIR.

CLARINS RETRACTABLE BROW DEFINER IN LIGHTEST BROWN
HER PENCILED-IN, SEVERELY-ARCHED BROWS WERE HER OTHER TRADEMARK.

JEAN HARLOW

In less than a decade, Jean Harlow made an indelible mark in Hollywood, becoming the very first blonde bombshell (Marilyn was, in fact, number two). And the movie that catapulted the young, curvaceous actress to superstardom was Howard Hughes's production about World War I dogfighters, *Hell's Angels* (1930). Hughes cast the then little-known actress in his big budget film as Helen, the object of two brothers' affections, and offered the public the only color scenes of Harlow in film history. Despite enduring tragedy in her personal life—second husband Paul Bern committed suicide shortly after they were married—she went on to find success and a knack for comedy in movies like *Bombshell* (1933) and *Dinner at Eight* (1933). Harlow fought and won the battle to be seen as more than a sex symbol, though her overwhelming sensuality was hard to ignore—she never wore underwear and would rub ice around her nipples before filming a scene. Sadly her star didn't shine for long—Harlow died suddenly during the filming of her final movie, *Saratoga* (1937), at twenty-six years old, a victim of kidney disease. Max Factor said after her passing, "She was simply the twentieth century's most influential person in the world of beauty. She has set a style that will be copied for years to come."

MARY PICKFORD

YVES SAINT LAURENT BABY DOLL
SHE WAS AMERICA'S FAVORITE LITTLE DOLL, AND THIS SWEET SCENT WOULD HAVE SUITED HER PERFECTLY.

SEPHORA FALSE LASHES
FOR MUCH OF PICKFORD'S CAREER, HER EYES HAD TO DO THE TALKING.

MATRIX CURL.LIFE BODY SHAPING FOAM
ONE OF HER NICKNAMES WAS "THE GIRL WITH CURLS," SO MANE MAINTENANCE WAS IMPORTANT.

Mary Pickford was one of the most prolific actresses of her time, appearing in close to 250 films—176 of them by the time she reached the age of twenty. The petite (barely five feet tall), curlicued doll was recognized worldwide as "America's sweetheart," not only for her sweetness on the screen in films like *Rags* (1915), *Little Annie Rooney* (1925), and her first "talkie," *Coquette* (1929), for which she won an Oscar, but also for her work off set. Pickford made huge strides for women in Hollywood—she helped establish the Motion Picture Relief Fund; and was one of the founders of United Artists with Charlie Chaplin, D.W. Griffith, and the man who would become one of her three husbands, Douglas Fairbanks; was the first female actor to earn more than a million dollars in a year; and the first to produce and supervise her own films. With all her achievements on- and off-screen, it is fitting that Pickford was the first star to officially place her hand and footprints outside Los Angeles's famed Grauman's Chinese Theater.

1940s &'50s

War caused a seismic shift in beauty ideals. Widespread makeup shortages and changing attitudes about the vanity which characterized the prior decades led to a desired appearance that was more pure than provocative. The look of popular pinups like Rita Hayworth and Betty Grable was wholesome and affable, a far cry from the exotic beauties of the '20s and '30s. But after the war ended, women wanted to reclaim their femininity and steep themselves in elegance. Beauties like Elizabeth Taylor and Ava Gardner epitomized the new ideal, along with campaigns like the one for the Revlon fragrance Fire & Ice, which bore the famous tagline "For the woman who plays with fire and skates on ice."

ELIZABETH TAYLOR
in *Cat on a Hot Tin Roof*

Often regarded as one of the most beautiful women in the world, Elizabeth Taylor started her film career at a tender age, appearing opposite animals in *Lassie Come Home* (1943) and *National Velvet* (1944). There were no animals co-starring with her in 1958's *Cat on a Hot Tin Roof*, the film adaptation of Tennessee Williams's famous play, which showed the full breadth of the young actress's beauty. She played the feisty "Maggie the Cat," stuck in a tumultuous marriage to Brick (a ruggedly handsome Paul Newman), and the story chronicles their ups and downs within a larger, dysfunctional Southern family. Taylor looked magnificent from start to finish, her raven hair cut in short curls, her lashes heavy, and her pout painted a glossy apricot hue. The actress was just as irresistible in her personal life, accruing a grand total of seven husbands, twice marrying Richard Burton, and famously stealing Eddie Fisher from America's sweetheart Debbie Reynolds. Taylor accepted her weakness for men: "What do you expect me to do? Sleep alone?" she once asked. Besides being known for a list of failed marriages, Taylor has in recent years made headlines because of another odd relationship: her friendship with Michael Jackson.

ELIZABETH TAYLOR WHITE DIAMONDS EAU DE TOILETTE
THIS WOMAN WOULD HAVE NO QUALMS ABOUT DOUSING HERSELF IN HER OWN FRAGRANCE.

DUWOP VIOLET EYES
THE PERFECT COLOR PALETTE FOR A WOMAN KNOWN FOR HER STRIKING VIOLET EYES.

CHRISTIAN DIOR ROUGE LONG-WEARING CREAMY LIP-COLOR IN ANGELIC CORAL
IT WAS TAYLOR'S SIGNATURE SHADE THROUGHOUT THE MOVIE.

LAUREN BACALL

LANCÔME COLOR DESIGN LIPSTICK IN EN VOGUE
BACALL IS THE ONLY LEGEND WHO IS MENTIONED IN MADONNA'S FAMOUS HIT "VOGUE" AND STILL VERY MUCH ALIVE.

GARNIER FRUCTIS STYLE SOFT CURL CREAM
BACALL'S SMOOTH WAVES WERE ENTICING FOR BOTH HER FANS AND BOGIE.

SMASHBOX COSMETICS BROW TECH IN BLONDE
HER FAMOUSLY ARCHED BROWS WERE THE ACCENTS ON HER LOVELY FACE.

The stars surely must have been aligned on the set of 1944's *To Have and Have Not*, for it was there that Bacall and Bogie met and fell madly in love. It was the first film role for nineteen-year-old Bacall, the only child of Jewish immigrants (a fact she hid early on due to a fear of anti-Semitism). She had been handpicked by director Howard Hawks's wife (who saw her on the cover of *Harper's Bazaar* magazine) to play Marie "Slim" Browning. The husky-voiced starlet was swiftly nicknamed "the Look," for her slyly raised brow and the curls she would purposely let cascade over one side of her face. The chemistry between Bacall and Bogart was palpable in *To Have and Have Not*, and would be rekindled on-screen in *The Big Sleep* (1946), *Dark Passage* (1947), and *Key Largo* (1948), and off-screen, when the two married in 1945. Though the pair's incredible love story would come to an end in 1957, when Bogart died of throat cancer, Bacall, or as he called her, "Baby," is still wooing audiences to this day.

ELIZABETH ARDEN COLOR INTRIGUE LIPSTICK IN DRAMA
TURNER HAD JUST AS MUCH DRAMA IN HER PERSONAL LIFE AS SHE DID ON-SCREEN.

RIMMEL PROFESSIONAL EYEBROW PENCIL
SINCE HER ORIGINAL BROWS WERE SHAVED OFF FOR A ROLE IN HER YOUTH, A GOOD PENCIL WAS A NECESSITY.

CONAIR IONIC CERAMIC STYLER 1875
LEGEND HAS IT THAT WHEN THERE WAS A FIRE IN HER APARTMENT YEARS AGO, SHE GRABBED THREE ITEMS: A HAIR-DRYER, LIPSTICK, AND HER EYEBROW PENCIL.

LANA TURNER

Allegedly discovered perched at the counter of her local ice-cream parlor while still in high school, Turner debuted on-screen in the original *A Star is Born* (1937), and—ahem—developed the nickname "Sweater Girl" after appearing in some form-fitting wool that same year in *They Won't Forget*. The buxom, bottle blonde (she actually had auburn hair) was an obvious pinup for soldiers in World War II, and after the war, that same sultry demeanor made her a perfect star for a string of sexy on-screen romances, including the film noir *The Postman Always Rings Twice* (1946) opposite John Garfield and *The Bad and the Beautiful* (1952) with Kirk Douglas. Despite earning critical acclaim for *Peyton Place* (1957) and *Imitation of Life* (1959), Turner's career success was overshadowed by the intense spectacles in her personal life—"I planned on having one husband and seven children, but it turned out the other way around." Besides a lifelong struggle with alcohol and multiple failed marriages, Turner had to contend with a troubled daughter, who in the late '50s fatally stabbed Turner's mobster lover (a crime for which she was eventually acquitted).

OLAY ORIGINAL ACTIVE HYDRATING BEAUTY FLUID
FOR A WOMAN THIS LOW MAINTENANCE, EVEN FACE CREAM WAS A LUXURY.

CREST WHITESTRIPS
HER PERFECT TEETH ENDURED THROUGHOUT HER LONG LIFE.

PANTENE PRO-V RED EXPRESSIONS DAILY COLOR ENHANCING SHAMPOO IN AUBURN TO BURGUNDY
HEPBURN LIVED UP TO THE REDHEAD STEREOTYPE WITH HER FIERY PERSONALITY.

KATHARINE HEPBURN

For Katharine Hepburn, the record holder for number of Best Actress Oscar wins (three), stardom was simply a fact of life. Born to progressive New England parents—her mother was a well-known suffragette who helped Margaret Sanger found what would become Planned Parenthood—the bright, athletic Hepburn was raised with a strong sense of independence that would endure throughout her life. After graduating from Bryn Mawr with a dual degree in history and philosophy, she began to work on Broadway before making the jump to Hollywood. Though her '30s-era performances in films like *Morning Glory* (1933), *Little Women* (1933), and *Bringing Up Baby* (1938) were celebrated, Hepburn really gained her reputation for her refusal to acquiesce to Hollywood standards. At around 5' 8", she literally towered above her female peers, refused to trade in her mannish slacks for dresses ("I wear my sort of clothes to save me the trouble of deciding which clothes to wear"), despised makeup, and was unabashedly outspoken. But while Hepburn may have been unconventional in life, on film she was a unanimous hit—she garnered a total of twelve Oscar nods, including ones for *The Philadelphia Story* (1940), *Woman of the Year* (1942), where she met her longtime love Spencer Tracy, and *The African Queen* (1951). Hepburn once said, "I'm a personality as well as an actress. Show me an actress who isn't a personality and you'll show me a woman who isn't a star."

MODELCO TAN AIRBRUSH IN A CAN
"THERE ARE TWO REASONS WHY I AM SUCCESSFUL IN SHOW BUSINESS AND I AM STANDING ON BOTH OF THEM."

CALVIN KLEIN OBSESSION EAU DE PARFUM SPRAY
SHE WAS A TRUE ALL-AMERICAN GIRL, MUCH LIKE THIS SCENT.

POUT LIP POLISH IN BUXOM BETTY
SHE ALWAYS HIGHLIGHTED EVERY POSSIBLE ASSET.

BETTY GRABLE

Betty Grable was thrust into the limelight by an overzealous mother and encouraged to lie about her age so she could begin working in her early teens. Her first film appearance was as a chorus girl in *Whoopee!* (1930), and though she would appear in close to fifty films in that decade, it was the '40s that cemented her star status. Grable was as American as apple pie with her blonde curls and peachy complexion, and it was this look that would propel her pinup status during World War II. The image of the dizzy blonde in a bathing suit smiling over her shoulder with her hands on her hips showed off the asset that boosted soldiers' spirits and earned her more accolades than her acting: absolutely perfect gams. Long before Jennifer Lopez reportedly had her famously full derriere insured, Grable had a million dollar premium taken out on her legs by Lloyd's of London. And though she was charming in a number of '40s-era musical comedies like *Sweet Rosie O'Grady* (1943) and *Pin Up Girl* (1944), Grable was always aware of her own limitations—"I'm a song-and-dance girl. I can act enough to get by. But that's the limit of my talents."

LANCÔME AQUA FUSION TEINTÉ IN NATUREL
LIKE MOTHER, LIKE DAUGHTER—ONE OF BERGMAN'S TWIN CHILDREN, ISABELLA ROSSELLINI, WAS THE FACE OF THE BRAND FOR FOURTEEN YEARS.

FACE STOCKHOLM ADVANCED HYDRATION VITAMIN CREAM
THE SWEDES ALWAYS ADORED BERGMAN, AND SHE WOULD HAVE SURELY APPRECIATED THIS LINE FROM HER BIRTHPLACE.

ACQUA DI PARMA COLONIA
ITALY WAS HER ADOPTED HOME FOR A TIME, SO SHE WOULD HAVE LOVED THIS CLASSIC SCENT FROM THE "BOOT."

INGRID BERGMAN

Ingrid Bergman is one of the most revered actresses of the twentieth century, and though it was always her talent that was celebrated, beauty this resplendent is impossible to overlook. A Swedish actress, the shy Bergman first turned heads opposite Humphrey Bogart in the romantic classic *Casablanca* (1942), which depicted the two as former lovers whose flame is rekindled amidst the chaos of World War II, a role she is still best recognized for. She went on to star in and garner awards for a number of other parts in such movies as *For Whom the Bell Tolls* (1943), *Gaslight* (1944), and *Joan of Arc* (1948). Besides the movie-going American public, Bergman also famously made Alfred Hitchcock weak in the knees—the director was so smitten with the statuesque Swede that he cast her in a trio of films: *Spellbound* (1945), *Notorious* (1946), and *Under Capricorn* (1949). But Hollywood can be a cruel and hypocritical place, a fact the reserved actress discovered after she was blacklisted following her decision to abandon her family and begin a relationship with Italian director Roberto Rossellini. Despite being ostracized for her immoral behavior, she was able to win crowds over again with her Oscar-winning 1956 role in *Anastasia*—"I've gone from saint to whore and back to saint again, all in one lifetime." And for that, we can only make a nod to Bogart and say, "Here's looking at you, kid."

CHANEL ROUGE ALLURE LIPSTICK IN SEXY
"SEX APPEAL IS FIFTY PERCENT WHAT YOU'VE GOT AND FIFTY PERCENT WHAT PEOPLE THINK YOU'VE GOT."

VINCENT LONGO LA DOLCE VITA LASHES
AT THE HEIGHT OF LOREN'S POPULARITY, LIFE WAS INDEED SWEET.

BOBBI BROWN LONG-WEAR GEL EYELINER IN BLACK INK
LOREN'S EYES WERE ALWAYS ELONGATED WITH THE HELP OF JET-BLACK LIQUID LINER.

SOPHIA LOREN

The illegitimate daughter of Romilda Villani and Riccardo Scicolone, Sophia Loren was born into poverty during wartime in Italy, a situation that would mirror the setting of the movie that would earn her a little gold statue. Surprisingly, the Italian actress known for her dangerous curves was actually nicknamed "Toothpick" as a child for her scrawny frame caused by war-era hunger; as she later joked, "Everything you see, I owe to spaghetti." Well, the carbo-loading paid off because once Loren filled out, she became a voluptuous stunner who went from regional beauty contests to Hollywood movies, playing opposite some big-time stars, like Frank Sinatra in *The Pride and the Passion* (1957), Cary Grant in *Houseboat* (1958), and Tab Hunter in Sidney Lumet's sexy *That Kind of Woman* (1959). Though always resplendent on-screen, Loren's most memorable role was one that showcased her acting abilities over her bodily assets. Loren's performance in 1960's *Two Women* as a heartbroken mother trying to protect her daughter during World War II was so exacting that she earned an Academy Award, the first ever presented for a performance in a foreign-language film.

GOODY FLOWER BARRETTE
CARMEN'S SIGNATURE FLOWER WAS TUCKED BEHIND DANDRIDGE'S EAR WHEN SHE GRACED THE COVER OF *LIFE* MAGAZINE, ANOTHER FIRST FOR AN AFRICAN-AMERICAN WOMAN.

STILA GEL CHEEK COLOR IN MELON FLUSH
THIS IMITATES A NATURAL FLUSH BEAUTIFULLY.

BUMBLE AND BUMBLE CURL CONSCIOUS CURL CREME IN KINKY CHICK
KEPT HER HEAD-TURNING CURLY COIF IN PLACE.

DOROTHY DANDRIDGE in *Carmen Jones*

Had Dorothy Dandridge been born in another era, she would have had a better chance at a long, illustrious acting career. But in the '40s and '50s, prejudice often overshadowed promise for young African-American actresses—as she herself once pointed out, "If I were white, I could capture the world." Dandridge's love for the stage began as a child, performing in Baptist churches with her sister, and led to small, stereotyped parts on the big screen. Hollywood's lack of desirable roles for black actresses didn't keep her out of the spotlight, and she stayed busy singing at nightclubs around the country. *Carmen Jones* (1954), a cinematic version of Bizet's opera *Carmen* with an all-black cast, was a major break for Dandridge. Her performance garnered an Oscar nomination for Best Actress, the first ever in that category for an African-American actress. As the lead, the elegant beauty was transformed into the fiery, sultry Carmen, with shiny black waves, and flushed cheeks and lips that had all the men in heat. Dandridge's own life was rife with misfortune—she died from barbiturate poisoning at the age of 41, two years after declaring bankruptcy. She reportedly had $2.14 in her account.

TARTE LIP GLOSS IN RHETT & SCARLETT
THIS RED GLOSS WILL HAVE SUITORS WHO DO GIVE A DAMN LINING UP AROUND THE BLOCK.

ALMAY GREEN EYE PALETTE
THE PERFECT SHADES TO COMPLEMENT HER FAMOUS GREEN EYES.

SO PRETTY BY CARTIER EAU DE TOILETTE
ADVERTISED AS A FRAGRANCE FOR A WOMAN OF GRACE CHARM, LEIGH WC HAVE LOVED CART LUSH FLORAL.

VIVIEN LEIGH
in *Gone with the Wind*

Vivien Leigh was a proper English actress who achieved international acclaim for playing a Southern belle…twice. She began her career in British plays and films, including 1937's *Fire Over England*, where she met and fell for co-star Laurence Olivier. Both eventually left their respective spouses and embarked on an intense love affair that would endure for twenty years and would see the pair cast together on both stage and screen. Leigh was extremely selective about her roles—she famously refused a secondary part in *Wuthering Heights*, saying she was only interested in the lead—and was determined to play Scarlett O'Hara in *Gone with the Wind* (1939). Her resolve paid off, and Leigh's turn as the defiant Southern belle oppos Clark Gable's debonair Rhett Butler during the unres of the Civil War earned her an Oscar and rave review For a woman who was accustomed to receiving prais more for her delicate beauty than her acting, this wa a major achievement. Though *Gone with the Wind* w a career high point for the petite, raven-haired actre she went on to give first-rate performances in *Water Bridge* (1940), *Anna Karenina* (1948), and *A Streetc Named Desire* (1951), for which she earned her seco Oscar. While many of Leigh's peers considered her to be difficult, her chronic mood swings would later be attributed to a lifelong battle with manic depression

JUDY GARLAND
in *A Star Is Born*

Judy Garland might have been the first child star damaged by the Hollywood machine, a less-than-illustrious distinction garnered from starting a performing career at the oh-so-fragile age of three, as part of a family vaudeville act. Signed to a contract with MGM at twelve, the cherubic actress had a series of bit parts before, at age sixteen, landing the role of Dorothy in *The Wizard of Oz* (1939), a part that would define her as one of Hollywood's great singing stars. "Over the Rainbow," sung with her signature pure, shivering voice, became both a timeless hit and a prophecy of sorts—"I wanted to believe and I tried my damndest to believe in the rainbow," she once said. "I tried to get over and couldn't." Garland, who constantly struggled with her weight and an addiction to pills, would marry and divorce twice before making a phenomenal comeback in the aptly titled remake of the late thirties film, *A Star Is Born* (1954). Clad in the simplest suits, her character of Esther the showgirl was a vision, fresh-faced and demure, a far cry from the drama of Garland's personal life. She lost the Oscar that year to Grace Kelly, and her own life just over a decade later to an accidental overdose of barbiturates.

CARON POWDER PUFF
THE SECOND STAR OF THE FILM WAS HER LUMINOUS SKIN.

STELLA ROSE ABSOLUTE FRAGRANCE
GARLAND, WHOSE FAVORITE FLOWER WAS THE ROSE, POSTHUMOUSLY HAD A SPECIAL VARIETY NAMED AFTER HER.

RIMMEL RICH MOISTURE CREAM LIPSTICK IN RED HOT
BOTH GARLAND AND HER DAUGHTER, LIZA, HAVE A PENCHANT FOR A CRIMSON POUT.

JAYNE MANSFIELD

Born Vera Jane Palmer, this bodacious blonde studied acting at college in Texas while racking up local beauty-queen titles before making her screen debut with a bit part in *Female Jungle* (1954) as, here's a real stretch, a buxom blonde. Mansfield entered show biz during a time when Marilyn Monroe, due to personal problems, was falling out of favor, so many saw her as a ditzy blonde replacement—"A forty-one-inch bust and a lot of perseverance will get you more than a cup of coffee…a lot more." Though she usually stuck to B-movie fare, Mansfield did have two hits, as a gangster's gal in *The Girl Can't Help It* (1956) and as a sex symbol with a sense of humor opposite Tony Randall in *Will Success Spoil Rock Hunter?* (1957). Her life off-screen was always much more eventful than her movie career—she had three husbands, five children, multiple affairs, and the infamous "Pink Palace," a mansion she shared with second husband Mickey Hargitay that was decorated from floor to ceiling in various shades of rose. But Mansfield's life ended in a tragedy so horrific it seemed only fit for the movies—in 1967, while on U.S. Highway 90 near New Orleans, the car she was riding in with three of her children was struck by a tractor trailer, an incident chronicled years later in the Siouxsie and the Banshees song "Kiss Them for Me." Her children survived; she did not.

VICTORIA'S SECRET HOTTEST BODY UPLIFTING BUST TREATMENT
SHE WAS THE FIRST (LEGIT) AMERICAN ACTRESS TO SHOW OFF HER BIRTHDAY SUIT ON THE BIG SCREEN IN THE AMERICAN FILM, *PROMISES! PROMISES!* (1963).

PLAYBOY BEAUTY KISSING GLOSS IN FIRST KISS
MANSFIELD WAS A *PLAYBOY* PLAYMATE OF THE MONTH IN 1955. "I LIKE BEING A PINUP GIRL. THERE'S NOTHING WRONG WITH IT."

AGENT PROVOCATEUR FRAGRANCE
"IF YOU'RE GOING TO DO SOMETHING WRONG, DO IT BIG, BECAUSE THE PUNISHMENT IS THE SAME EITHER WAY."

RITA HAYWORTH

Rita Hayworth, aka "The Love Goddess," was actually born Margarita Carmen Cansino to a family of famous Spanish dancers. Rita Cansino, a trained dancer herself, started her Hollywood career as the exotic raven-haired Spanish señorita in a string of '30s B movies, before getting electrolysis around her hairline to push it back, dyeing it red, and becoming Rita Hayworth. She starred in films like *The Strawberry Blonde* (1941) with James Cagney, *You'll Never Get Rich* (1941) with Fred Astaire, and *Cover Girl* (1944) opposite Gene Kelly before landing the lead in *Gilda* (1946), the role that would define her image and secure her place in movie history forever after. The saucy redhead femme fatale was alluring in every scene of that classic film noir, even shocking censors with a racy one-glove striptease. Though she wooed many off-screen—and was such a popular wartime pinup that her face was reputedly glued to an A-bomb—Hayworth never fancied herself a sexual icon. According to Hayworth, "Men go to bed with Gilda, but wake up with me."

PRADA TENDRE FRAGRANCE
HAYWORTH ONCE SAID, "I NEVER THOUGHT OF MYSELF AS A SEX GOD-DESS, MORE A COMEDIAN WHO COULD DANCE." THIS SULTRY PERFUME MIGHT HAVE MADE HER COMFORTABLE WITH HER FEMME FATALE IMAGE.

BIOTHERM BUST'UP INTENSIVE BUST FIRMING GEL
WHEN ASKED WHAT KEPT HER SEXY STRAPLESS DRESS IN PLACE DURING THE FILMING OF *GILDA*, SHE RESPONDED, "TWO THINGS."

CLAIROL HERBAL ESSENCES BOLD N' BRILLIANT COLOR IN CHILEAN SUNSET
HAYWORTH, WITH HER FAKE RUBY MANE AND SULTRY DEMEANOR, INSPIRED THE RED-OB-SESSED WHITE STRIPES' RECENT HIT "TAKE TAKE TAKE," OFF THEIR ALBUM *GET BEHIND ME SATAN.*

GENE TIERNEY

Gene Tierney may have been born into privilege—she spent time at finishing schools in Europe, and her wealthy parents had her on the socialite track—but much of her life was marred by eerie tragedy reminiscent of the film noir that made her famous. After dabbling in modeling and stage acting in New York, the beauty with the slight overbite and prominent cheekbones made her Hollywood debut opposite Henry Fonda in the western *The Return of Frank James* (1940). She shined in a string of films in the '40s and '50s like *Heaven Can Wait* (1943), *Leave Her to Heaven* (1945), and *Where the Sidewalk Ends* (1950), but is best recognized for her turn as the murdered girl in the noir mystery *Laura* (1944). Tierney's Laura was a living doll, with shoulder-grazing curls, pursed bow-tie lips, and mysterious eyes, and the public fell in love with her. But off-screen, Tierney's life was unraveling. She gave birth to a mentally retarded child after contracting German measles from an overzealous fan during a USO tour, and her grief led to a lifelong battle with manic depression. Tierney was treated with electroshock therapy and tried to commit suicide by jumping from a ledge in 1957. The ravishing actress would eventually succumb to emphysema, a disease caused by the cigarette addiction she picked up on the set of her first film after she was told her voice was too high.

LANCÔME COLOR DESIGN IN RETRO ROUGE
THIS "RETRO" CRIMSON IS JUST THE SHADE LAURA WOULD HAVE WORN.

BOURJOIS TALONS ALGUILLES MASCARA IN NOIR
THE DARK, MOODY LIGHTING OF THE TYPICAL FILM NOIR CALLS FOR A POWERFUL, RICH MASCARA.

CHANEL COCO EAU DE PARFUM
AFTER SPENDING TIME POLISHING HER LANGUAGE SKILLS ABROAD, TIERNEY SPOKE PERFECT FRENCH.

JULIE HEWETT LIPSTICK IN FEMME NOIR
THE REQUISITE SHADE FOR ANY GODDESS OF THE GENRE.

REVLON RED NAIL POLISH
REVLON'S SCARLET POLISHES WERE VERY MUCH IN FASHION.

VERSACE CRYSTAL NOIR FRAGRANCE
THIS PAIRING OF GARDENIA AND AMBER IS AN INTRIGUING COMBINATION OF SEXY AND INNOCENT.

AVA GARDNER in *The Killers*

Born into a poor Southern family of tobacco farmers, Gardner saw Hollywood as her way out. Though she appeared in a slew of films during the '40s, Gardner made headlines for her personal life before her movie roles—she married Mickey Rooney at age nineteen in 1941 and was divorced less than two years later. The statuesque, green-eyed beauty cemented her role as a major sex symbol in the 1946 film noir classic *The Killers*, based on the short story by Ernest Hemingway. As the sultry, mysterious Kitty Collins, Gardner was gorgeous in revealing body-hugging gowns, sporting shiny dark-brown curls, creamy skin, and scarlet lips. While she was never celebrated for her acting chops, she delivered *The Killers'* memorable one-liners like, "I'm poison, Swede, to myself and everybody around me," with ease, and had a few more impressive roles, especially in *Mogambo* (1953) and *The Night of the Iguana* (1964). The public stayed interested in Gardner's personal life—she had a rocky marriage to Frank Sinatra and an affair with Howard Hughes—even after she retreated to a life abroad. Though she died in her sixties, the brazen star once declared, "I wish to live until 150 years old, but the day I die, I wish it to be with a cigarette in one hand and a glass of whiskey in the other."

NATALIE WOOD
in *Rebel Without a Cause*

VO5 SHEER! HAIRDRESSING WEIGHTLESS LEAVE-IN CREAM
WOOD'S SHORT BOB WAS CURLED TO PERFECTION FOR HER REBEL ROLE.

SHISEIDO EYEBROW AND EYELINER COMPACT IN DEEP BROWN
WOOD WAS KNOWN FOR HER PLATTER-SIZED EYES AND THE THICK BROWS THAT FRAMED THEM.

HARD CANDY CHARMED LIP GLOSS BRACELET
BECAUSE OF A SLIGHT BONE PROTRUSION ON HER LEFT WRIST FROM A CHILDHOOD ACCIDENT, SHE ALWAYS WORE A BRACELET.

Natalie Wood started her long acting career as a toddler, when the diminutive daughter of Russian-Orthodox immigrants landed her first role in 1943's *Happy Land*. Wood once opined, "In so many ways, I think it's a bore to be sorry you were a child actor—so many people feel sorry for you automatically. At the time I wasn't aware of the things I missed, so why should I think of them in retrospect? Everybody misses something or other." She worked on more than twenty films as a child, best remembered as the girl who doesn't believe in Santa Claus in *Miracle on 34th Street* (1947). The precocious actress was still a teenager when she landed the role of a lifetime in 1955's *Rebel Without a Cause*, starring opposite the heartthrob James Dean as the good girl wooed by the town rebel, a role carried off with such aplomb that she was nominated for the first in a series of Oscars. She later starred in *Splendor in the Grass* (1961) and *West Side Story* (1961) before her tragic, untimely death, which remains shrouded in mystery to this day. Wood, who had a lifelong fear of drowning, died in 1981 after tumbling from a yacht she had been relaxing on with husband Robert Wagner and actor Christopher Walken.

THREE CUSTOM COLOR LIP GLOSS IN BILLIE
HER VOICE WAS SO AN-GELIC THAT THE BAND L DEEMED HER THE "ANG OF HARLEM" IN THEIR FAMOUS SONG.

FRESH SATIN LUSTER FACE PALETTE
ONE OF HER MOST FAM HITS WAS "LADY IN SATI

JO MALONE VINTAGE GARDENIA COLOGNE
BILLIE HOLIDAY'S SIGNA-TURE ACCESSORY WAS A FRAGRANT GARDENIA FLOWER TUCKED BEHIN HER EAR.

BILLIE HOLIDAY

Billie Holiday (born Eleanora Fagan) had a troubled life from the very beginning. Her grandfather was one of seventeen children of a white plantation owner and a black slave; she was born to a thirteen-year-old mother and a jazz-musician father who jumped ship when Billie was an infant. Shuffled between relatives and angry in general, Holiday first became enamored with the music of Louis Armstrong and Bessie Smith when she was running errands for a Baltimore brothel. Soon enough, the aspiring performer was warming up her vocal cords at Harlem jazz clubs. After being discovered in the '30s, Holiday (or Lady Day, as she was known to the masses) would go on to record hundreds of songs like "Strange Fruit" and "God Bless the Child" over the next two decades and perform alongside jazz legends like Count Basie and Artie Shaw, making strides both for women and African-Americans in the music business. But drugs would cut Holiday's stardom short, roughing up her voice and personal life. She once said, "Dope never helped anybody sing better or play music better or do anything better. All dope can do for you is kill you—and kill you the long, slow, hard way." And it did.

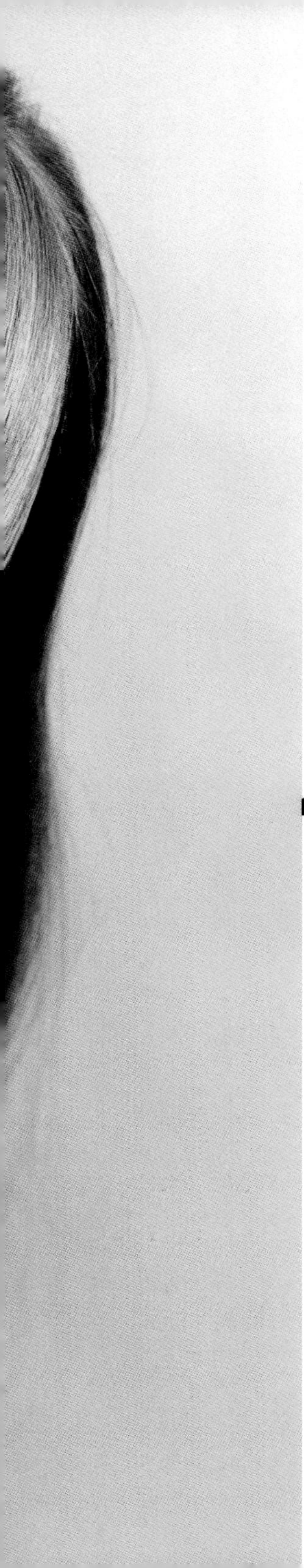

1960s

The sixties were a decade of rebellion—from the simultaneous Civil Rights and antiwar movements, to the psychedelic music, to the outrageous fashion trends (Rudi Gernreich's topless bathing suit!), to the rising popularity of psychotropic drugs. And that same defiant spirit extended into the world of beauty. The '60s paradigm of beauty was either audacious (Marianne Faithfull, Claudia Cardinale) or slightly adolescent (Twiggy, Edie Sedgwick). Hair was long and loose, or shorn into pixie-like cuts, and faces were either bare and sun kissed, or adorned with long, false lashes, and thickly lined lids. In the decade of free love, the theory for beauty was simple: anything goes.

MICHELLE PHILLIPS

"California Dreamin'" was one of the most iconic tunes of the decade, but besides defining a generation, it also ignited the career of Michelle Phillips, the waifish blonde who co-wrote the song with her then husband and fellow band-member John (a credit that no doubt garners her many royalties to this day). The two married when she was barely eighteen, and formed a band called The Magic Circle, which included Denny Doherty and Cass Elliott, who Michelle reportedly first met while tripping on acid. (They changed their name to the Mamas and the Papas in 1965.) The band's reign as America's musical response to the British Invasion was brief—a mere four years of writing and recording. But surprisingly, the downfall wasn't drugs; it was infidelity. Michelle had been carrying on an affair with Doherty, which would ruin both her marriage and the band—it has been said that Mama Cass was furious because she herself was in love with Doherty. After getting fired, Michelle deepened the wound by dating Gene Clark of rival band The Byrds. Though they would all reconcile, it was never the same. While Michelle's solo musical career never gained steam, she did use her quintessential good looks for television, most famously as Valerie's mom on *Beverly Hills 90210*. But her musical legacy lived on for a time in her daughter Chynna, who formed the band Wilson Phillips in 1989 with the two daughters of Beach Boy Brian Wilson.

MURAD OIL-FREE SUNBLOCK
SHE LOOKED LIKE THE QUINTESSENTIAL CALIFORNIA GIRL, JUST MINUS THE SUN DAMAGE.

FRESH INDEX PATCHOULI PURE EAU DE PARFUM
LIKE IT OR NOT, PATCHOULI REMAINS THE ICONIC HIPPIE SCENT.

LAURA MERCIER EYE COLOR IN TEMPTATION
DENNIS HOPPER WAS SO TEMPTED BY THE SWEET BLONDE THAT HE MARRIED HER FOR EIGHT DAYS IN 1970, A TIME MICHELLE REFERS TO AS "THE HAPPIEST DAYS OF MY LIFE."

CATHERINE DENEUVE
in *Belle de Jour*

YSL BAUME NOURRISSANT MOISTURIZING LIP AND NAIL BALM
DENEUVE, WHO WAS DRESSED FOR HER ROLE IN *BELLE DE JOUR* BY YVES SAINT LAURENT, WAS THE LEGENDARY DESIGNER'S MUSE FOR MANY YEARS.

LANVIN ARPEGE
DENEUVE MAY HAVE HAD A BRAND OF PERFUME NAMED AFTER HER, BUT HER SEX-CRAZED CHARACTER WOULD HAVE LUSTED AFTER THIS SENSUAL SCENT.

CHANEL INIMITABLE MASCARA
DENEUVE BECAME THE FACE OF CHANEL FOR A TIME IN THE '70S.

In France, Catherine Deneuve is a bona fide national treasure. The delicately beautiful blonde actress is so beloved in her native country that she was one of the models for Marianne, the symbol of the French republic (an honor also held by both Brigitte Bardot and, more recently, Laetitia Casta). Acting was already a family business when Deneuve started—her elder sister, Françoise Dorléac, was a successful French film actress, who died tragically in a car crash in the sixties. Deneuve first swept her fellow citizens off their feet in the musical *The Umbrellas of Cherbourg* (1964), but her turn as the unsatisfied married woman with bedroom eyes and tousled hair who works part-time as a prostitute in Luis Buñuel's *Belle de Jour* (1967) made her an international star. As Séverine Serizy, Deneuve transformed daily from chaste housewife to an insatiable masochist who prostituted herself using the pseudonym Belle de Jour. The French actress was also unconventional in her personal relationships—she had two children out of wedlock with directors Roger Vadim and Marcello Mastroianni, and once claimed, "I don't see any reason for marriage when there is divorce."

Marianne Faithfull was still a teenager when she recorded the song that would both launch and define her career. The daughter of an Austro-Hungarian aristocratic mother and a former British military officer who ran a commune in Oxfordshire, the petite songstress with honey-blonde hair grew up in England with nobility in her blood. Faithfull was famously discovered by producer Andrew Loog Oldham at a party thrown by the young Rolling Stones, and supposedly was initially turned off by the now-legendary rockers. Her aversion didn't last long—Mick Jagger and Keith Richards penned the sleepy ballad "As Tears Go By" and introduced her smoky voice to the world in 1964. And after a short-lived marriage to artist John Dunbar, with whom she has a son, Nicholas, Faithfull's relationship with Jagger became more than just professional. The gorgeous pair was the perfect picture of London's swinging sixties and carried on a very public, and often very tumultuous, relationship throughout the decade. At the time, the young Faithfull not only garnered fans for her music, but also for her acting in films like *Girl on a Motorcycle* (1968) and *Hamlet* (1969). Heroin would eventually sabotage her already capricious relationship with Jagger, and even threatened to cut short her career, but Faithfull recovered, and re-emerged on the music scene in the late '70s.

ANNA SUI SHADOWS IN 004 AND 005
HAD ANNA SUI BEEN AROUND IN THE SWINGING SIXTIES, SHE SURELY WOULD HAVE DEFINED THE LOOK.

LANCÔME ROUGE SENSATION IN NATURAL
SHE FAVORED A NUDE, FLESH-TONED LIP OVER DEEPER SHADES.

PAUL LABRECQUE STRAIGHT GLOSSING CREAM CONDITIONER
FAITHFULL'S SIGNATURE LOOK IN THE SIXTIES WAS LONG, STICK-STRAIGHT HAIR WITH A HEAVY FRINGE FRAMING HER FACE.

MARIANNE FAITHFULL

ANNA KARINA

GUERLAIN KISS KISS LIPSTICK IN ENVIE DE BEIGE
KARINA FOUND THE MOST FAME IN FRANCE.

BVLGARI POUR FEMME PERFUME
KARINA WOULD WIN AWARDS FOR HER PORTRAYAL OF ANGELA IN *UNE FEMME EST UNE FEMME*.

M.A.C TECHNAKOHL LINERS IN GRAPH BLACK AND GREYPRINT
FOR A NEW WAVE FILM ACTRESS, BLACK-RIMMED EYES ADDED A NECESSARY ELEMENT OF MOODINESS.

Anna Karina, born in Denmark, started her career as a cabaret singer before moving to Paris at age eighteen. It was there, in true Cinderella style, that the slender, gamine beauty was discovered by fashion designers Pierre Cardin and Coco Chanel, who promptly convinced her to change her name from Hanne Karin Blarke Bayer to the catchier Anna Karina. She first met Jean-Luc Godard, the man who would define her career, in the late '50s, when he was a journalist for *Cahiers du Cinema*. After turning down Godard's first film offer, *À Bout de Souffle* (1960), because of a nude scene, the two worked together in 1961's *Une Femme est Une Femme*, and were married that year. Their on-screen collaboration would be more successful than their personal one (they got divorced in 1968), yielding seven exciting films and transforming Karina into the darling of the Nouvelle Vague cinema. Though she would work on a number of other films, it was the French New Wave pairings with Godard that she is best remembered for—in addition to her turn as Angela, the nightclub singer who wants to have a baby, in *Une Femme est Une Femme*, she was also unforgettable as Marianne in the sexy red dress theorizing about love in *Pierrot Le Fou* (1965), and as the frigid Natacha learning about emotions and conscience in the sci-fi-esque *Alphaville* (1965).

She never did look like much of a Bancroft—the esteemed actress was in fact born Anna Maria Louisa Italiano to a pair of Italian immigrants in the Bronx. Bancroft, who always wanted to be on stage, changed her name for her debut in the 1952 film, *Don't Bother to Knock*, after being told that her given name was too "ethnic." She chose Bancroft because it sounded elegant. While her acting career thrived on screen (*The Pumpkin Eater* and *The Miracle Worker*) and on stage (*Two for the Seesaw* and *The Miracle Worker*) and earned her acclaim and awards—she is on a short list of those who have won an Oscar, an Emmy, and a Tony—it was her role in 1967's *The Graduate* that made her an icon. Bancroft played Mrs. Robinson, a scandalously older, married woman who seduces a recent college grad only to watch him fall in love with her daughter. (Dustin Hoffman, who played the title role, was actually only six years younger than Bancroft.) The film was an instant classic, and besides cementing Bancroft's and Hoffman's star statuses, the soundtrack also propelled the career of folk duo Simon and Garfunkel with the song "Mrs. Robinson."

SHU UEMURA EYELASHES
BEDROOM EYES WOULD NOT BE COMPLETE WITHOUT A PAIR OF FALSE LASHES.

EAU SAUVAGE BY CHRISTIAN DIOR EAU DE TOILETTE
HER LIPS MAY BE SAYING "I'M NOT TRYING TO SEDUCE YOU," BUT HER FRAGRANCE IS SAYING SOMETHING ELSE.

YSL MAKE-UP LEG MOUSSE
THOUGH IT WAS THE LEG OF LINDA GRAY (FUTURE STAR OF *DALLAS*) THAT APPEARED ON THE FAMOUS MOVIE POSTER FOR *THE GRADUATE*, BANCROFT STILL NEEDED SOME SHIMMER DURING FILMING FOR HER OFT-EXPOSED GAMS.

ANNE BANCROFT in *The Graduate*

She may have been named after child star Shirley Temple, but the similarities between the two actresses end with their matching red hair. Born Shirley Beaty (her brother is actor Warren Beatty), MacLaine first made her way to New York not to become an actor, but a dancer. Part of a chorus line, she was plucked from obscurity to replace Carol Haney on Broadway in *The Pajama Game*. Soon after, MacLaine made her screen debut in Hitchcock's *The Trouble with Harry* (1955), and starred with fellow members of the infamous Rat Pack (she was often considered the group's one female associate) in *Artists and Models* (1955) and *Ocean's Eleven* (1960). But it was opposite Jack Lemmon in *The Apartment* (1960) that MacLaine really showed off her acting chops. Director Billy Wilder's follow-up to *Some Like It Hot* saw a fresh-faced, pixie-topped MacLaine as Miss Kubelik, an attractive elevator operator involved in an illicit affair. The chemistry between her and the young Lemmon was electric, and led to Oscar nods for both and a win for best picture. MacLaine's acting career is still going strong and she has had a number of notable post-*Apartment* roles—as an optimistic taxi dancer in *Sweet Charity* (1969), a meddling mother in *Terms of Endearment* (1983), and the potty-mouthed, cynical Ouiser in *Steel Magnolias* (1989).

SHIRLEY MACLAINE in *The Apartment*

MICHAEL KORS LEG SHINE IN SHIMMER
MACLAINE ONE CLAIMED, "I WAS NEVER A GREAT BEAUTY. I WAS NEVER A SEX SYMBOL. I DID, HOWEVER, HAVE GREAT LEGS BECAUSE I WAS A DANCER."

FRÉDÉRIC FEKKAI GLOSSING SHINE MIST
TO KEEP HER RICH AUBURN HUE SHINY.

COVER GIRL FANTASTIC LASH WATERPROOF MASCARA
MISS KUBELIK SHED HER FAIR SHARE OF TEARS BEFORE LEMMON'S CHARACTER SWEPT HER OFF HER FEET.

ESTÉE LAUDER PURE COLOR LIPSTICK IN MELON
THIS WAS ANITA'S SIGNATURE SHADE.

PHYTO CURL ENHANCING SHAMPOO
HER CROPPED CURLY POODLE CUT SUITED HER BOISTEROUS PERSONALITY PERFECTLY.

DR. HAUSCHKA ROSEMARY LEG AND ARM TONER
MORENO'S LEGS GOT JUST AS MUCH OF A WORKOUT IN *WEST SIDE STORY* AS HER VOCAL CHORDS.

RITA MORENO in *WEST SIDE STORY*

Rita Moreno, born Rosita Dolores Alverio in Puerto Rico, was an anomaly in Hollywood, a petite Hispanic actress amid a sea of blondes. Though she found early success as a teenager doing Spanish voice-overs and some Broadway plays, once she arrived in Tinseltown, she was relegated to roles she found demeaning. Moreno got her big break playing Anita in the film version of Leonard Bernstein and Stephen Sondheim's *West Side Story* (1961), a story loosely based on Shakespeare's *Romeo and Juliet*. *West Side Story* was landmark for several reasons: it had a darker theme than its musical predecessors, incorporating thorny social issues into the plot; it showcased the talent of Hispanic actors like Moreno in glamorous, leading roles; and it produced a number of hit songs like "Somewhere" and "America." *West Side Story* would collect ten Academy Awards, more than any other musical in history, including a best supporting actress prize for Moreno. It would be the first of many trophies for the sassy, dark-haired actress—she has reached the entertainment zenith by accruing an Oscar, a Tony, an Emmy and a Grammy. And she is still going: she was the voice of the title character on the children's TV show *Where on Earth is Carmen Sandiego?*, and had a role on the gritty HBO prison drama *Oz*.

EDIE SEDGWICK

Edie Sedgwick was the embodiment of sixties decadence and rebellion. Born into a tony New England family, the leggy, wide-eyed bottle blonde was the quintessential "poor little rich girl" who abandoned her fortune to embark on a life a little less, well, ordinary. Sedgwick found instant stardom as a model—she was one of *Vogue's* famous "youthquakers" in '65 earning extra praise for her "legs to swoon over"—but it was as a member of Warhol's clan of the beautiful and bizarre that she found superstardom. She quickly became his muse and constant companion, appearing in a slew of his underground films (*Vinyl*, *Kitchen*, and *Chelsea Girls*) and becoming the queen to his king of the Manhattan nightlife. Truman Capote once posited, "Andy Warhol would like to have been Edie Sedgwick...a charming, well-born debutante from Boston." With her inimitable style—the freakishly long legs that were often clad in just black tights and topped with a boatneck shirt and gargantuan earrings—and delightfully maniacal ways (she almost burned down the famous Chelsea Hotel), everyone wanted to be, or at least be next to, Edie. In her time, Bob Dylan and the Cult both penned songs that allegedly paid homage to her ("Just Like a Woman" and "Ciao, Edie," respectively); today, she continues to fascinate, having inspired the recent movie *Factory Girl*. But Sedgwick was too much, too fast, and, as tragic as it was, her untimely passing from a barbiturate overdose was no surprise.

M.A.C LASHES
SEDGWICK WAS SO OBSESSED WITH HAVING A HEAVY CURTAIN OF LASHES THAT SHE WOULD OFTEN LAYER ONE SET OF FALSE LASHES OVER ANOTHER.

MALLY CITY CHICK SMOKEY EYE KIT
SEDGWICK'S EYES WERE ALWAYS POSITIVELY COATED IN INKY SHADOWS, A TECHNIQUE THAT SHE WOULD SPEND HOURS IN FRONT OF THE MIRROR PERFECTING.

DIOR ROUGE LONG WEARING CREAMY LIPCOLOR IN INGENUE PINK
A LIGHT FROSTED LIP OFFSET HER DONE-UP EYES.

MAYBELLINE NEW YORK WATERPROOF ULTRA LINER IN BLACK
HER EYES WERE CONSTANTLY COATED WITH SEXY BLACK LINER.

DOLCE & GABBANA SICILY
ALTHOUGH SHE GREW UP IN TUNISIA, CARDINALE'S ROOTS ARE SICILIAN.

MATRIX VAVOOM EXTRA-FULL FREEZING HAIRSPRAY
CARDINALE'S HAIR WAS PURE SIXTIES: LONG AND BIG.

CLAUDIA CARDINALE

When Claudia Cardinale won the title of the Most Beautiful Italian Girl in Tunisia in 1957, she could barely speak a word of the language. Though her parents were Italian, she was raised in North Africa, and French was her mother tongue. After catching a glimpse of the ravishing brunette, the Italian film industry was understandably intrigued—she made her screen debut in *Goha* (1958), starred opposite Burt Lancaster in *Il Gattopardo* (1963), and won acclaim for her role in *La Ragazza di Bube* (1963). But her role in *8½* (1963) was pivotal in more ways than one. Not only is Federico Fellini's Oscar-winning masterpiece widely considered one of the best films of all time, but it also introduced the world to Cardinale's real voice. Her previous Italian films had all been dubbed due to her beginner's grasp of the language, but Fellini appreciated her unique French-accented Italian, and, of course, her sexy deep voice. But with her long dark hair, curvaceous figure, and warm smile, Cardinale was so devastatingly beautiful in the dreamy, Proustian black-and-white film that she could have spoken with a lisp and it wouldn't have mattered. She once quipped, "If you're not English, then you're a foreigner—so you must be sexy. It's an old British cliché."

1970s

If the seventies had a representative face, it would certainly be the king of bizzarro himself, David Bowie. Each of his album covers during those years (*Aladdin Sane*, *Diamond Dogs*, and *The Rise and Fall of Ziggy Stardust*) raised the bar for fashion and beauty eccentricities. And eccentric was the decade's motto. There was a renewed passion for bright, over-the-top hair and makeup (YSL's No. 19 fluorescent fuchsia lipstick was a favorite), something missing since the freewheeling '20s, and androgyny gained street cred thanks to stars like Bowie and Grace Jones. Beauty was loud, exotic, and, most importantly, totally glam.

BARBRA STREISAND
in *The Owl and the Pussycat*

L'ORÉAL SUBLIME GLOW DAILY MOISTURIZER
STREISAND'S GETUPS IN THIS FILM LEFT MOST OF HER BARE.

I.D. BARE ESCENTUALS GLIMMER IN PUSSYCAT
THIS PUSSYCAT'S GLOW DIDN'T NECESSARILY COME FROM MAKEUP.

FACE STOCKHOLM INDIVIDUAL FALSE LASHES
ADDED TO THE OUTE CORNERS, FALSE LASHES ELONGATE THE EYE BEAUTIFULL

If show business had a poster girl, it would undoubtedly be Brooklyn-born Barbra Streisand. Though she was reportedly discouraged from going into the business by her mother, who thought she wasn't pretty enough, that didn't stop her. Streisand, or "Babs," as she is affectionately known by legions of fans, first took the stage in her teens as a nightclub singer in Greenwich Village gay bars—she probably had no idea back then that she would eventually become an icon in the gay community alongside entertainers like Bette Midler and Judy Garland—and eventually made a name for herself on Broadway in *Funny Girl*. Streisand's turn in the 1968 film version earned her her first Oscar, which she shared with Katharine Hepburn (the only tie for Best Actress in Academy history) Though she was widely acclaimed for *Funny Girl*, seeing her dirtier side as Doris, the coarse but charming hooker in the 1970 comedy *The Owl and the Pussycat*, is obviously intriguing. Named after an 1871 nonsens cal children's poem by Edward Lear, it was a successful Broadway play before its transformation into a film If Streisand's sex appeal was ever questioned, the role of Doris laid that to rest. In the words of Mike Myers's famous Babs-loving *Saturday Night Live* character Linda Richman, her performance was "like buttah."

O.P.I NAIL LACQUER IN CALL MY CELL-ERY
THE DEEP EMERALD SHADE ACCENTUATED HER JAZZ HANDS ONSTAGE.

DIANE BRILL LASH LINGERIE
HOW CAN A STARLET BAT HER EYES PROVOCATIVELY WITHOUT THEM?

MAYBELLINE NEW YORK MOISTURE EXTREME LIPCOLOR IN ROYAL RED
A SHOWGIRL IS JUST NOT MUCH OF A SHOWGIRL WITHOUT THE REQUISITE RED LIPS.

LIZA MINNELLI in *Cabaret*

Liza Minnelli, the daughter of the legendary Judy Garland and director Vincente Minnelli, first got her taste of the limelight as a toddler opposite Mom in the movie *In the Good Old Summertime* (1949). Minnelli was hooked, and she began her career on the New York stage, earning her first Tony Award in 1965 at age nineteen for *Flora, the Red Menace*. Named after the Gershwin song Garland often sang in concert, "Liza (All the Clouds'll Roll Away)," Minnelli quickly proved that she was just as talented as her mother...and just as fabulous. As Sally Bowles, the American entertainer in Weimar Republic-era Berlin, in Bob Fosse's much-beloved and often-reinterpreted musical *Cabaret* (1972), Minnelli was, in the words of her own character, "divine decadence, darling!" Onstage at the movie's Kit Kat Club, Bowles wore not much more than garters, a bowler hat, and a smile. Her makeup was, in true showgirl style, completely garish—think Kermit-green nails and an exaggeratedly painted face. Minnelli's own life was just as outlandish—she spent much of the '70s with friends like Halston at Studio 54, married David Gest in an affair more flamboyant than her husband (they divorced shortly after amid rumors that she beat him), and, most recently, spoofed her own kooky persona in a wickedly funny cameo on *Arrested Development*. Perhaps Bowles herself put it best: "That's me, darling. Unusual places, unusual love affairs. I am a most strange and extraordinary person."

M.A.C LIPSTICK IN DIVA
DIANA ROSS CAN STILL TURN HEADS... A FACT THAT BEAUTY GIANT M.A.C PROVED A FEW SEASONS AGO WHEN IT USED HER AS A MODEL FOR AN AD CAMPAIGN.

PAUL MITCHELL THICKEN UP STYLING LIQUID
TRACY'S HAIR WAS ALWAYS SHINY AND COIFFED.

VINCENT LONGO WATER CANVAS CRÈME-TO-POWDER FOUNDATION IN MAHOGANY
ROSS'S SMOOTH, DARK SKIN EARNED HER CHARACTER THE NICKNAME "MAHOGANY."

DIANA ROSS
in *Mahogany*

Place Diana Ross on any stage, and she will effortlessly live up to the "legend" moniker. And the *Guinness Book of World Records* would concur—in 1993, it named her the most successful female recording artist of all time, thanks to her eighteen number-one singles (six on her own, the rest with the Supremes). While she may have a serious set of pipes, Ross's star quality also resonated on-screen. She pulled off Billie Holiday with both grace and gravitas in 1972's *Lady Sings the Blues*, and was an absolute vision alongside Billy Dee Williams in 1975's *Mahogany*. Slender and wide-eyed, Ross played Tracy (nicknamed Mahogany because she is "dark, beautiful, rich and rare"), a girl from the Chicago ghetto with dreams of becoming a fashion designer. Tracy found fame and fortune but traded it all for—you guessed it—love.

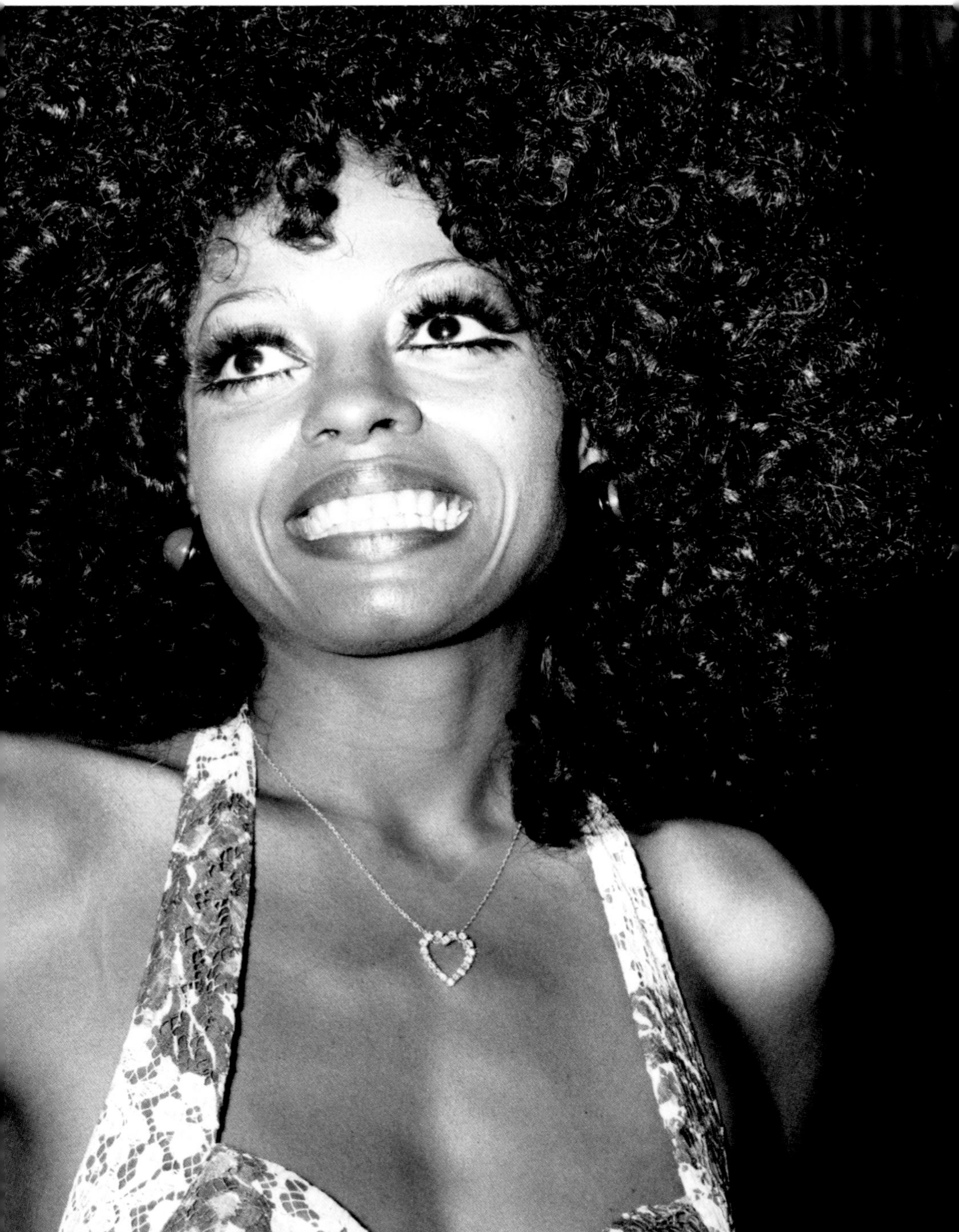

FAYE DUNAWAY in *Chinatown*

Faye Dunaway looks like a movie star should—perfect bone structure, long sun-kissed hair, and parallel rows of gleaming white teeth. But this Southern girl didn't make a name for herself with red-carpet-ready looks alone. After spending a number of years in New York theater, Dunaway first made waves on screen as Bonnie opposite Warren Beatty's Clyde in the 1967 film that chronicled the exploits of the famous criminal duo. Though her acting was laudable enough to earn her an Oscar nomination, her beauty was equally impossible to ignore—Bonnie was hands down the foxiest bank robber in history, sporting a shiny bob plus cocked berets, ballet flats, and pencil skirts. She was equally smoldering in *The Thomas Crown Affair* (1968), but it was Roman Polanski who transformed her into the ultimate femme fatale in 1974's *Chinatown*. The homage to '30s-era film noirs saw Dunaway as the frosty Evelyn Mulwray opposite a trim Jack Nicholson as the cynical private eye Jake "J.J" Gittes. Evelyn's makeup was a throwback to the days of Clara Bow—dramatic, fake brows; a Marcel wave; and dark, bow-tie lips—and was inspired by Polanski's memories of his mother's beauty routine. Though nominated again for her role as Evelyn, Dunaway would have to wait two more years for an Oscar—she won for her portrayal of a ball-stomping company exec in 1976's *Network*.

LORAC CREAMY BROW PENCIL IN BLONDE
TO ACCURATELY EMULATE THE '30S STYLE, BROWS MUST BE DRAWN ON DRAMATICALLY.

T3 TWIRL CURLING IRON
THIS WAVE REQUIRES A GOOD CURLING IRON AND STEADY HANDS.

LAURA MERCIER LIP COLOUR IN GARNET
EVELYN'S CHOSEN COLOR WAS DARK AND ALLURING.

VINCENT LONGO LIPSTAIN LIPSTICK IN FOOLISH VIRGIN
THOSE WHO HAVE NEVER EXPERIENCED A LIVE *ROCKY HORROR* SHOW ARE CALLED "VIRGINS"; THOSE WHO HAVE ONLY SEEN THE MOVIE ARE "MASTURBATORS"; AND THE REGULARS ARE "SLUTS."

TRESEMMÉ TOUCHABLE CURLS SHAPING MILK
SARANDON'S CROWN OF RINGLETS ADDED TO HER INNOCENT APPEAL.

RED FLOWER JAPAN OHANA GINGERGRASS BAMBOO SCRUB
JANET SPENT THE VAST MAJORITY OF THE MOVIE CLAD ONLY IN A BRA AND SLIP SO SMOOTH SKIN WAS A NECESSITY.

SUSAN SARANDON in *The Rocky Horror Picture Show*

Susan Sarandon's big break as an actress came when she was busy pursuing her other passion: political activism. While at the 1968 Democratic National Convention with then husband and fellow drama student Chris Sarandon (whose surname she still uses professionally), she was plucked from a sea of hippies to play a major role in *Joe* (1970) as the rebellious teen daughter. Though the curvy, strawberry-blonde actress is now best known for dramas like *Thelma & Louise* (1991) and *Dead Man Walking* (1995), it was the 1975 comedy-horror musical *The Rocky Horror Picture Show* that set Sarandon's career into orbit. She played Janet, the naïve newlywed who, along with her new husband, Brad (Barry Bostwick), finds herself in a secluded castle with a gender-bending scientist from the planet Transsexual (Tim Curry) and his peculiar (to put it mildly) cast of characters. With outrageous musical numbers and a whole lot of humor, the film graphically showcased a long list of shocking taboos, from incest to homosexuality to voyeurism. Though it was widely panned by critics at the time, *Rocky Horror* is now the ultimate cult classic and is the highest-grossing movie to have never played in more than two hundred theaters at the same time. Now Sarandon often uses her voice for a very different project: peace demonstrations.

GRACE JONES

Grace Jones is one of those stars who is famous less for her artistic abilities, and more because she simply couldn't avoid the spotlight—this Jamaican goddess was born notorious. Not surprisingly, Jones's exquisitely long limbs and chiseled features were in high demand in the modeling industry, though she often found more success in Paris, where a severe look like hers was appreciated. But it didn't matter; Jones was never interested in being merely a hanger for designer clothes. After securing a deal with Island Records, the androgynous beauty recorded a trio of disco albums—*Portfolio* (1977), *Fame* (1978), and *Muse* (1979)—and her outrageous, raucous live performances became widely popular, particularly in the gay community. Jones resurrected the Edith Piaf classic "La Vie en Rose," was a regular on the Studio 54 circuit, became a friend and muse to Andy Warhol, and developed a reputation for wild behavior. "I've always been a rebel," she once said. "I never do things the way they're supposed to be done. Either I go in the opposite direction, or I create a new direction for myself."

NARS FAME LIPSTICK PALETTE
JONES PAINTS HER LIPS WITH FOUR DIFFERENT SHADES OF LIPSTICK, SO AN EXTENSIVE PALETTE IS IMPORTANT.

BOND NO. 9 NEW HAARLEM FRAGRANCE
FORGET FLORALS. IN FACT, FORGET WOMEN'S FRAGRANCES ALTOGETHER.

M.A.C PIGMENTS IN ROSE GOLD, COPPER SPARKLE, AND STEEL BLUE
JONES HAS NO FEAR WHEN IT COMES TO COLOR AND, WELL, FOR THAT MATTER, ANYTHING ELSE.

ANNA SUI FRAGRANCE
NICKS, WHO SHARES ANNA SUI'S FREE-SPIRITED STYLE, WOULD HAVE LOVED THIS DREAMY BULGARIAN ROSE SCENT.

ORIGINS GOLD DUST EYESHADOW
NICKS PENNED THE SONG "GOLD DUST WOMAN" ON FLEETWOOD MAC'S SECOND ALBUM.

URBAN DECAY SURREAL SKIN LIQUID MAKEUP CONCEALER IN DREAM
NICKS HAS ALWAYS BEEN ATTRACTED TO THE MYSTICAL (THOUGH NOT WITCHCRAFT, AS SOME WOULD BELIEVE), SO SHE WOULD BE ENAMOURED WITH THIS GENIE BOTTLE OF "SURREAL" FOUNDATION.

The future chanteuse born Stephanie Lynn Nicks first met Lindsey Buckingham in the halls of a California high school. While still teenagers, the two formed a band with two other musicians called Fritz, which became popular enough to get them gigs opening for Creedence Clearwater Revival, Janis Joplin, and Jimi Hendrix. But because the petite, flaxen-haired Nicks garnered the most attention, Fritz was no more after 1971. Nicks and Buckingham released a record together which may have bombed, but it did grab the attention of Mick Fleetwood, who invited the pair, now lovers, to join Fleetwood Mac. Their first self-titled album as a group was a hit, thanks in large part to Nicks's insightful songwriting ("Rhiannon" and "Landslide") and a voice that had an exceptional purity. And the follow-up *Rumours* was an even more massive success, spurning the group's only *Billboard* number-one single, "Dreams," and selling more than eighteen million copies. As a solo artist and as part of Fleetwood Mac, Nicks would go on to have many more hits far beyond the '70s, but it was the gypsy with the long blonde waves, pouty lips, layers of hippie garb, and tambourine in hand that inspired a host of imitators.

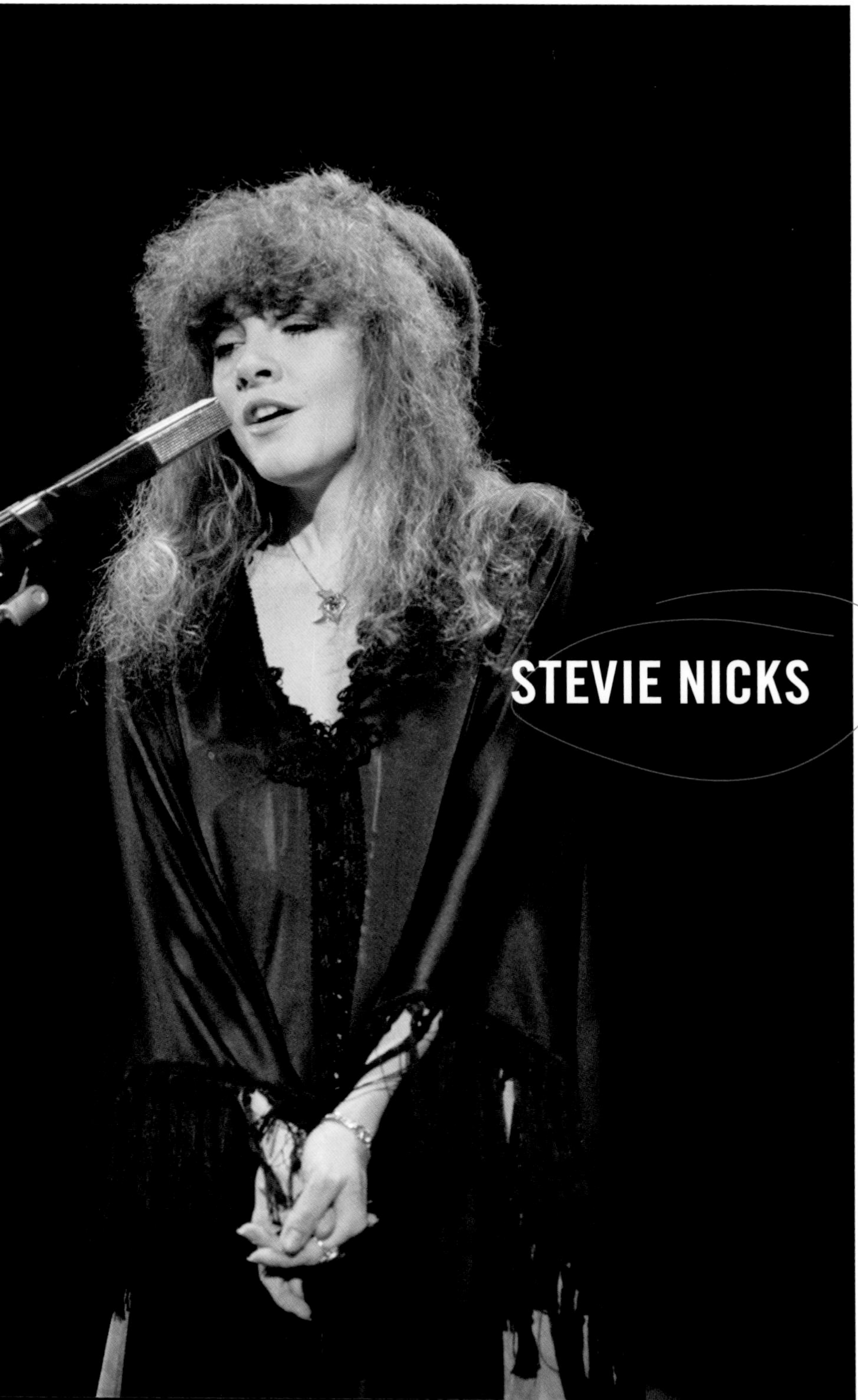
STEVIE NICKS

KIEHL'S ORIGINAL MUSK BLEND NO. 1 FRAGRANCE SHE WAS THE VOICE OF EQUALITY, SO SHE WOULD LOVE A STRONG UNISEX SCENT.

DUWOP HANDS 2 HAIR NEVER ONE TO BE HIGH MAINTENANCE, STEINEM WOULD APPRECIATE THIS DUAL-PURPOSE CREAM.

ELIZABETH ARDEN CERAMIDE PLUMP PERFECT MAKEUP 15 IN WARM SUNB ARDEN WAS AN EAR FEMINIST HERSELF.

GLORIA STEINEM

Gloria Steinem is the most recognized—and arguably the most gorgeous—feminist ever. After graduating magna cum laude from Smith College in 1956, the budding writer and activist spent time in London and India before embarking on a career in journalism in the States. Despite determination and an excellent education, Steinem found it difficult to break into the male-dominated magazine world; the article that is said to have helped was a 1960 exposé for *Show* called "I Was a Playboy Bunny." She went on to cofound both *New York* and *Ms.* magazines, and embarked on her career as a prolific feminist activist. Besides making (and continuing to make) great strides for women, and coining some of the most famous feminist one-liners ("A woman without a man is like a fish without a bicycle"; "The truth will set you free, but first it will piss you off"), Steinem became the decade's most unlikely style icon. Legions of girls were inspired not only by her powerful mantras, but also by her sun-kissed glow, the blonde streaks in her straight hair, and, of course, the tinted aviators.

PAM GRIER in *Coffy*

Pam Grier was the reigning queen of exploitation film—in fact, the entire exploitation genre might not have existed without her. After getting a rocky start in some hardcore women-in-prison flicks, Grier found her footing as the good-girl-gone-bad heroine in a string of '70s blaxploitation movies. The most memorable was *Coffy* (1973), in which Grier plays a dutiful nurse by day and vigilante by night who begins a bloody mission of revenge

CAROL'S DAUGHTER TUI HAIR OIL
TO KEEP THE 'FRO SHINY AND IN CHECK.

MAYBELLINE MOISTURE EXTREME LIPSTICK IN COFFEE GLAZE
THERE WAS ABSOLUTELY NO SUGAR IN THIS COFFY.

COVER GIRL QUEEN COLLECTION POWDER FOUNDATION IN SHEER TOFFEE
COFFY'S MOVES WERE AS SMOOTH AS HER SKIN.

on inner-city drug dealers and pimps, after her little sister gets exposed to contaminated heroin. Though some would see the pursuit of justice through violent means as necessitating a utilitarian look, that's not the case for Coffy. Grier's famously bodacious ta-tas are on full display in a variety of slinky getups throughout the film, as well as her equally bodacious Afro, which at one point doubles as the hiding place for a few razor blades. Though she may have been the object of many a man's fantasy in the disco era, nowadays Grier is busy being wooed by the fairer sex on Showtime's *The L Word*.

MAKE UP FOR EVER 12 GREASE PAINT CASE
THE RAINBOW OF CREAMY COLORS IN THIS BACKSTAGE STAPLE WOULD HAVE BEEN GREAT FOR RE-CREATING THE KABUKI STYLES HE PICKED UP FROM JAPANESE THEATER STAR TOMASU BORU.

CHRISTIAN BRETON NAIL POLISH IN NIGHT RAIDER
BOWIE ALWAYS CHOSE BLUE FOR EVERYDAY WEAR.

L'ORÉAL COLOR PULSE MOUSSE IN COPPER BLAST
THE INSPIRATION FOR HIS ORANGE-RED DYE JOB WAS A MASAYOSHI SUKITA PHOTOGRAPH IN A 1971 ISSUE OF *HONEY* MAGAZINE.

DAVID BOWIE as Ziggy Stardust

David Bowie has been dubbed a style icon too many times to count, but few have paid homage to Bowie the beauty icon. And there is so much to honor—chiseled cheekbones sharp enough to cut glass; pronounced canine teeth; hair that, whether platinum or copper, spiky or slicked back, is always impeccable; and those foxy eyes. As the story goes, Bowie—whose natural eye color is blue—got in a fight over a girl with school chum (and future Bowie album cover artist) George Underwood in the early '60s. Their schoolyard scrap left the burgeoning rocker with a permanently dilated left pupil and two different-colored peepers: one blue, and one that hovers between brown and green. While his clothing has always been legendary (one-arm spandex suits anyone?), it was his Ziggy beauty routine that left an indelible impression, not merely because of his commitment to makeup—the man would spend hours kneeling before his mirror like an altar—but also his wild creativity. He painted delicate lightning streaks on his cheek and often-exposed upper legs, coated his lids with acidic shades of red and yellow, and then there was the infamous gold circle. Bowie's third eye was painted on his forehead with thick gold cake makeup and, when he was feeling extra special, outlined with tiny gold rhinestones. Bowie's look was artistic, over-the-top, and, best of all, totally impractical.

1980s

Eighties beauty was a study in contrasts. A new interest in fitness brought about a correspondingly fresh and natural appearance exemplified by women like Phoebe Cates and Christie Brinkley. While the hangover from the overstated styles of the seventies lived on in the flash-and-trash looks of Madonna and Cyndi Lauper, the one commonality, whether the style was simple or showy, was that it was all big. Just as shoulder pads inflated fashion's favorite silhouettes, "big" also made its way into beauty. Hair was teased to grandiose proportions, and lashes, lips, and breasts were all pumped up to maximum density. The decade's lasting lesson: bigger is not always better.

PHOEBE CATES

in *Fast Times at Ridgemont High*

Born and raised in New York City, Cates, whose exotic looks are thanks to parents of Russian and Chinese descent, was a teenage model before she made the transition to acting. She even graced the cover of *Seventeen* magazine, the era's teen-style bible. Coincidentally, Cates was that very age when she flaunted her birthday suit for the first time—"I was only seventeen when I did my nude scenes in *Paradise* (1982). They were serious and more difficult because they were not easily justified. But the topless scene in *Fast Times at Ridgemont High* (1982) was funny, which made it easy." Amusing for Cates, and arousing for every prepubescent boy in the country. As Linda, "the experienced girl," in Amy Heckerling and Cameron Crowe's landmark teen movie about life at a SoCal high school, she was the all-American teen dream. And the infamous scene—Cates slides out of the pool in a red bikini and slowly peels off her top in time with The Cars song "Moving in Stereo," all while locking eyes with the camera in a masturbatory dream sequence envisioned by Judge Reinhold's character—secured the movie's major box-office success.

LOVE'S BABY SOFT
THE YOUTHFUL, POWDERY SCENT WAS THE SIGNATURE OF MANY AN '80S GIRL.

NEUTROGENA BUILD-A-TAN GRADUAL SUNLESS TANNING LOTION
ALL CUTOFF-JEANS-WEARIN CALIFORNIA GIRLS IN THE EIGHTIES WERE TAN. WHITE WAS NOT HOT.

JEMMA KIDD MAKE UP SCHO LASTING TINT SEMI-PERMANENT WATERPROOF LASH COLOUR
BECAUSE EMERGING FROM POOL DRIPPING WET ISN'T A SEXY WHEN YOUR MASCARA RUNNING DOWN YOUR FACE

JOHN FRIEDA LUMINOUS COLOR GLAZE IN RADIANT RED
SHE WAS HANDS DOWN THE MOST FAMOUS REDHEAD OF THE DECADE.

TARTE SUPERGLOSS IN ANDIE & DUCKIE, TARTE LIPGLOSS IN JAKE & SAMANTHA
WONDER IF CLAIRE COULD HAVE DONE THE LIPSTICK TRICK WITH A GLOSS...

NARS LIPSTICK IN SCHIAP
RINGWALD'S POSITIVELY PINK-OBSESSED ANDIE WOULD HAVE BEEN OBSESSED BY THIS ELECTRIC SHADE INSPIRED BY THE CREATOR OF HOT PINK HERSELF, ELSA SCHIAPARELLI.

MOLLY RINGWALD

Molly Ringwald was the quintessential eighties teenager, in film after film after film. As Samantha Baker in *Sixteen Candles* (1984), her first major role, Ringwald, with her flat chest and flaming red hair, was a revelation for slightly awkward, insecure girls everywhere. *Candles* was director John Hughes's first in a string of teenage classics, and it is often considered the freshman effort from the "brat pack," of which Ringwald was a card-carrying member. Next up was the seminal teen-angst movie, *The Breakfast Club* (1985), which had the actress playing bitchy rather than the usual brainy, amongst her brat-pack cohorts. Besides capturing the plight of the troubled teen better than any other film at the time, it produced a host of one-liners ("Claire is a fat girl's name") and gave Simple Minds the biggest hit of their career, "Don't You (Forget About Me)." As precocious Andie in *Pretty in Pink* (1986) and troubled Jewel in *Fresh Horses* (1988), Ringwald found herself opposite eighties heartthrob Andrew McCarthy. Ringwald's post-teenage career never quite took off, and she once knowingly quipped, "You can't be sixteen forever." If only...

JEAN PAUL GAULTIER CLASSIQUE EAU DE PARFUM
GAULTIER WAS THE DESIGNER BEHIND HER INFAMOUS CONE BRA.

CHANEL ROUGE HYDRABASE CRÈME LIPSTICK IN MARILYN
MADONNA ALWAYS IDOLIZED MARILYN AND PAID THE LATE ACTRESS HOMAGE IN HER "MATERIAL GIRL" VIDEO, WHICH WAS BASED ON THE FILM *GENTLEMEN PREFER BLONDES.*

GARNIER 100% COLOR IN EXTREME ASH BLONDE
SHE HAD AN ENTIRE TOUR CALLED BLONDE AMBITION.

MADONNA

Madonna is a living legend, and it was during the eighties that she debuted, laying the groundwork for an entertainment career that has spanned decades and shows no signs of letting up. Born and raised in Detroit, Madonna lost her mother to cancer when she was only five, an event that has shaped her both personally and professionally. She moved from the Midwest to New York in the late seventies and struggled to support herself while pursuing a career in dance. It was during those tough years that Madonna began making music, and by 1982, she had two club hits with "Everybody" and "Physical Attraction." Her first self-titled album released in 1983 spawned hits like "Holiday," "Burning Up," "Borderline," and "Lucky Star," and gave the eager public its first peek at what would become the first of many style incarnations. Soon copycats everywhere were sporting the same wavy, blonde-streaked hair, red lips, rosaries, and stacks of black rubber bracelets. The same look endured for 1984's *Like a Virgin* album, which generated Madonna's most famous nickname ("Material Girl") and led to a lead role in the film *Desperately Seeking Susan* the following year. Always tweaking her look—she would chop off and bleach her hair for the androgynous *True Blue* (1986) days, and then go natural, and super-feminine for *Like a Prayer* (1989). Madonna once joked, "I am my own experiment. I am my own work of art."

ISABELLA ROSSELLINI in *Blue Velvet*

BOURJOIS PEARL EYESHADOW IN BLEU MYOSOTIS
IT WAS THE '80S, HENCE THE COPIOUS AMOUNT OF BLUE EYESHADOW.

GIVENCHY LIP LIP LIP! ESSENTIAL LIPSTICK IN DATING ROUGE
A WOMAN THIS SEDUCTIVE WOULDN'T JUST WEAR GLOSS.

DOLCE & GABBANA LIGHT BLUE PERFU
THIS FILM WAS MOST DEFINITELY HEAVY…VERY, VERY HEAVY.

Isabella Rossellini may have been born to act—her parents were Swedish actress Ingrid Bergman and Italian director Roberto Rossellini—but it took her years to discover it. She had a long and lucrative modeling career and even dabbled in Italian TV journalism before making her screen debut in the '70s. But by the time she appeared in David Lynch's 1986 twisted mystery-thriller *Blue Velvet*, she was certainly no novice. Every director has his or her tour-de-force film, and many cinophiles will argue that for Lynch, it's undoubtedly *Blue Velvet*. Upon returning to his hometown, impressionable college-boy Jeffrey (Kyle MacLachlan) discovers a severed human ear and is plunged into a cycle of sadomasochism, violence, and drug abuse…all in suburbia. Jeffrey's guide on his journey through depravity is mysterious nightclub chanteuse Dorothy Vallens, played with aplomb by a stunning Rossellini. To say Dorothy has baggage is an understatement—an ether-sniffing maniac (Dennis Hopper) has kidnapped her husband and child and is holding them ransom while he sexually humiliates her. Phew.

DIOR ROUGE VELVET LIPSTICK IN 30 AM
FOR A GIRL WHO TRULY BELIEVES THAT "NOTHING EXCEEDS LIKE EXCESS," NO CHEAP IMITATORS WILL SUFFICE.

EASY STRAIGHT PERFECT BLOW-OUT SPRAY
TO KEEP HER SLICK BOB LOOKING SHINY.

KEVYN AUCOIN THE GOSSAMER LOOSE POWDER
THE ONLY POWDER SHE WASN'T SHOVING UP HER NOSE.

MICHELLE PFEIFFER
n *SCARFACE*

Blonde-haired, long-limbed Michelle Pfeiffer is the quintessential California girl. But while her role in Brian De Palma's 1983 remake of the 1932 film *Scarface* was more vixen than Valley Girl, it was no less brilliant. *Scarface* became legendary for a number of reasons. It produced one of the best mob-movie catchphrases ever: "Say hello to my little friend." It showed gangsters who weren't Italian. And, most importantly, it introduced the world to ice-princess Elvira, Michelle Pfeiffer's best role to date (no, it's not *Dangerous Minds*). Set in '80s Miami, the film chronicles the rise of Cuban emigrant Tony Montana's drug-and-criminal empire. Gamine and glamorous, Elvira stood in stark contrast to Tony, for whom brash behavior and expletive-laced language were typical. Though sassy Elvira did get to fire back with her own set of one-liners, such as "Don't toot your horn, honey, you're not that good." By the end of the film, the body count had climbed to forty-two, both Elvira and Tony were full-fledged cokeheads, and the Montana empire had crumbled. But damn, she looked good.

CYNDI LAUPER

URBAN DECAY DELUXE EYESHADOWS IN FISHNET, GRAFFITI, AND ADORE
"YOU CAN'T STAMP OUT INDIVIDUALITY—THERE'S TOO MANY OF US."

YSL LIPSTICK NO. 19 FUCHSIA PINK
BECAUSE NO ONE HAS EVER CALLED HER NEUTRAL.

MANIC PANIC HAIR COLOR IN PILLARBO RED, ULTRA VIOLET, ATOMIC TURQUOISE, AND ELECTRIC LIZAR
LAUPER'S COLOR CH AREN'T FOUND IN YO TYPICAL DRUGSTORE AISLE.

Cyndi Lauper was responsible for the ultimate girl-power anthem, "Girls Just Want to Have Fun," and for an outrageous personal style that will forever be linked to the decade of excess. Born in Brooklyn, Lauper got her start performing in cover bands before forming the group Blue Angel, named after her favorite Marlene Dietrich film, in the late seventies. Though Lauper carved out a place for herself in the New York music scene, it wasn't until 1983's *She's So Unusual* that she gained widespread popularity. MTV put her lighthearted, colorful "Girls Just Want to Have Fun" video on heavy rotation, and suddenly multitudes of young women were emulating her colorful makeup and creative clothing. Besides the aesthetic influence, the album also produced hit singles with title track "She's So Unusual," ode to female masturbation "She Bop," and dreamy ballads "All Through the Night" and "Time After Time." The sweet-voiced petite singer followed up her success with *True Colors*, which while successful, was a lot quieter than her first effort and marked a giant step away from her punk-rock roots. While her musical career would never reach the same heights again, her fierce *Unusual*-era individuality remains an inspiration.

ESTÉE LAUDER ELECTRIC INTENSE LIPCREME IN DOLLY
"IT COSTS A LOT OF MONEY TO MAKE A PERSON LOOK THIS CHEAP."

BLISS GO BUST SUPER-SMOOTH BOOSTING FORMULA
"I DON'T KNOW IF THEY'RE SUPPORTING ME OR I'M SUPPORTING THEM."

GARNIER 100% COLOR EXTRA LIGHT NATURAL BLONDE
"I'M NOT OFFENDED BY DUMB BLONDE JOKES BECAUSE I KNOW THAT I'M NOT DUMB. I ALSO KNOW THAT I'M NOT BLONDE."

DOLLY PARTON

Dolly Parton is so revered that the first cloned mammal was named after her (Dolly the sheep), and there is an entire theme park, Dollywood, dedicated to her in Pigeon Forge, Tennessee. Not far from the amusement park in the Smoky Mountains, Parton grew up dirt poor, amongst twelve children in a one-room cabin. She started singing at an early age, and by thirteen had already signed a contract with a small record label and had performed at Nashville's Grand Ole Opry. Throughout the '60s and '70s, Parton established herself as an exceptional songwriter ("Jolene" and "I Will Always Love You") who melded elements of folk and country to great effect. The petite lady also established an exaggerated style featuring big hair and bigger boobs that became her signature: "I describe my look as a blend of Mother Goose, Cinderella, and the local hooker." Parton brought that same brassiness to her first film role. As Doralee, the dizzy Southern blonde in the comedy *9 to 5* (1980), she held her own opposite Jane Fonda and Lily Tomlin as they played working women exacting revenge on their sexist boss.

PRINCE

RIMMEL LYCRA LASH EXTEND
PRINCE IS VERY FAMILIAR WI
LYCRA PRODUCTS.

NARS LIP GLOSS IN ORGASM AND SCANDAL
"ORGASM" AND "SCANDAL" ARE TWO OF HIS FAVORITE WORDS.

HARD CANDY GLITTER EYE PENCIL IN GALAXY
ROCK BOYS SPORTING SMUDGED BLACK EYELINER ARE OLD HAT, BUT PRINCE IS CAREFUL TO WEAR HIS KOHL WITH A STYLE THAT IS MORE CLEOPATRA THAN KORN.

If androgyny had a spokesmodel, it would be Prince (birth name: Prince Rogers Nelson). From the *Controversy*-era bikinis, butt-free pants, and fingerless lace gloves, to *Purple Rain's* slim double-breasted aubergine suit and ruffled Victorian blouses, to the chunky heels he constantly wears not because he's short, but because "the ladies like 'em," Prince's style is more than just a little bit effeminate. Same goes for his beauty routine. His facial hair is usually groomed down to a preteen shadow, his curly coiffure tamed and slicked back, and though he sported lipstick only in his younger years, nowadays he is never without smoky eye makeup. Scandalous as his appearance might be on its own, when it is paired with erotically-charged lyrics and performances, the combination is totally lascivious, and, well, completely irresistible. Except maybe to Tipper Gore, who, after hearing her daughter playing "Darling Nikki" ("I met her in a hotel lobby / Masturbating with a magazine"), began her crusade for putting "explicit lyrics" labels on music. Thankfully, as far as we know, she never heard Prince's breathy panting on "Come" ("Don't be surprised if I make you my daily meal / Come/ Lickin' you inside, outside"), or we may have had more than just stickers to contend with. While Tipper may have been a hater, countless women have fallen prey to Prince's charms—both protégées (Sheila E., Vanity, and Carmen Electra) and reported lovers (Kim Basinger, Sherilyn Fenn, Sheena Easton).

MAGIC BY PRESCRIPTIVES ILLUMINATING POTION
HER SKIN HAS ALWAYS BEEN NATURALLY IMMACULATE.

DELUX BEAUTY LIPSTICK IN WILLIS
"WHAT'CHA TALKING ABOUT WILLIS?"

POUT BUSTIER BUST ENHANCING CREAM
TO SHOW OFF THE BEST BUST MONEY CAN BUY.

JANET JACKSON

Janet Jackson's surname is synonymous with entertainment and, more recently, with scandal—network television is still recovering from that infamous "wardrobe malfunction." The youngest of the nine-sibling musical clan, Jackson was first wooed (or pushed) onstage as a child by her legendarily domineering father on *The Jacksons* variety show, and proceeded to out-charm all of her brothers. Her acting caught the eye of Hollywood producers and led to memorable roles on *Good Times*, *Fame*, and as Willis's girlfriend, Charlene, on *Diff'rent Strokes*, but Jackson didn't give up the family business. Despite her initial hesitation for fear that she couldn't compete with her brothers, she recorded two albums, *Janet Jackson* (1982) and *Dream Street* (1984), in the early eighties that did fairly well. But it was only after she paired up with popular production duo Jimmy Jam and Terry Lewis for *Control* (1986) that the sexy singer became a star in her own right. The album produced five top-ten singles, and, thanks to choreographer Paula Abdul, established Jackson as a force to be reckoned with on the dance floor. Next up was *Rhythm Nation 1814* (1989), a musical masterpiece that made Jackson the only artist to earn seven top-five hits off the same album.

1990s

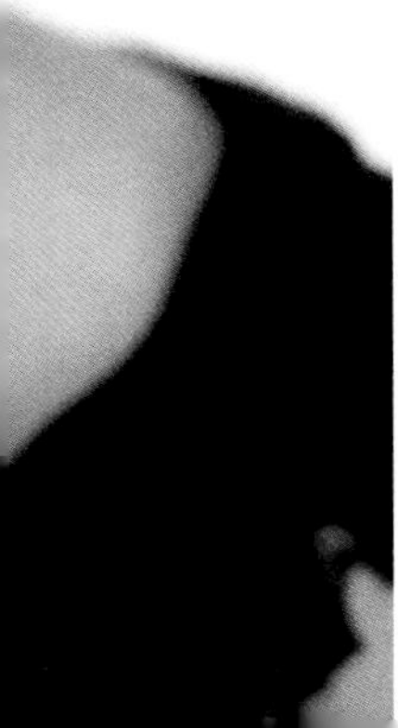

Grunge ruled the early nineties and waifish models like Kate Moss and Stella Tennant personified the much-admonished heroin chic. But besides being a decade of discontent, the '90s also marked a new interest in organic lifestyles—brands like Origins, Aveda, and the Body Shop touted natural products to great success. The rave scene moved up from the underground to produce colorful trends in hair, makeup, and accessories (pacifier, anyone?), and, eventually, bubblegum pop reached the beauty aisles as everything girly became *de rigueur*. Beauty became, above all, an accessory.

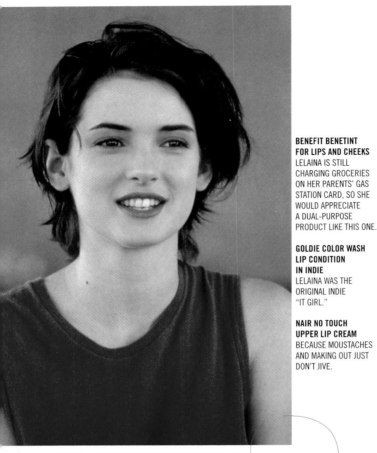

BENEFIT BENETINT FOR LIPS AND CHEEKS
LELAINA IS STILL CHARGING GROCERIES ON HER PARENTS' GAS STATION CARD, SO SHE WOULD APPRECIATE A DUAL-PURPOSE PRODUCT LIKE THIS ONE.

GOLDIE COLOR WASH LIP CONDITION IN INDIE
LELAINA WAS THE ORIGINAL INDIE "IT GIRL."

NAIR NO TOUCH UPPER LIP CREAM
BECAUSE MOUSTACHES AND MAKING OUT JUST DON'T JIVE.

WINONA RYDER in *Reality Bites*

Named after the town (Winona, Minnesota) where she was born, Winona Ryder was raised by counterculture parents on a commune in Northern California. The pale girl with the fragile features and chestnut eyes first started acting in the eighties, endearing audiences as the slouching Goth girl in *Beetlejuice* (1988), and alienating them as the most ferocious of the *Heathers* in the 1989 cult favorite opposite Christian Slater. But it was in the '90s that Ryder came into her own—she starred with then-boyfriend Johnny Depp in *Edward Scissorhands* (1990), was a God-fearing teen alongside a very young Christina Ricci in *Mermaids* (1990), and donned period costumes for both *Dracula* (1992) and *The Age of Innocence* (1993). In 1994, she was pitch-perfect as Lelaina, a confused aspiring videographer, in the slacker classic *Reality Bites*. Set in Houston, Texas, the film follows a group of friends as they try to navigate the post-college world of work and romance—Janeane Garofalo as the promiscuous Gap manager, Steve Zahn as the timid homosexual, Ben Stiller (also the film's director) as the smarmy corporate success story, and, last but certainly not least, Ethan Hawke as the brooding wannabe musician with a knack for losing jobs. *Reality Bites* defined Generation X's quarter-life crisis and made Winona Ryder a dream girl in the eyes of many an indie-rock boy.

LANCÔME JUICY WEAR LIPSTICK IN FOXY MAROON
THIS FOXY MAROON WOULD SUIT MIA PERFECTLY—HER SHORT-LIVED TELEVISION PILOT WAS CALLED FOX FORCE FIVE.

BOUCHERON TROUBLE FRAGRANCE
MIA, AND HER PENCHANT FOR STICKING THINGS UP HER NOSE, SPELLED TROUBLE FOR VINCENT VEGA.

L'ORÉAL FÉRIA MULTI-FACETED SHIMMERING HAIR COLOUR IN STARRY NIGHT
HER CLASSIC BROOKS BOB WAS DYED JET BLACK.

UMA THURMAN in *Pulp Fiction*

Uma Thurman was born in Massachusetts to progressive parents (her mom is a Swedish model turned psychotherapist once married to Timothy Leary, and her dad is an Indo-Tibetan Buddhist scholar) and named after a Hindu goddess. No surprise that the lanky, six-foot-tall, blonde-haired beauty with the serene face started modeling as a teen before beginning her film career. Prior to her role in *Pulp Fiction*, Thurman was best known for erotically charged parts in *Dangerous Liaisons* (1988) and *Henry & June* (1990), the first movie to acquire an NC-17 rating. But it was director Quentin Tarantino who would make Thurman a household name, casting her as gangster-girlfriend Mia Wallace in his 1994 hit. Tarantino tweaked the traditional crime-movie concept, borrowing heavily from French New Wave directors like Godard, and Italian spaghetti western director Sergio Leone. *Pulp Fiction's* explicit violence, unusual dialogue, motley crew of characters, and its overall campiness made it one of the most successful cult sensations of all time with both viewers and critics. And Thurman's slinky, witty Mia exuded a sly sexuality that recalled a younger Anna Karina, and provided the public with a host of one-liners, such as "I'll be there in two shakes of a lamb's tail."

MARC JACOBS BLUSH FRAGRANCE
DESIGNER MARC JACOBS DRAWS HEAVILY FROM THE GRUNGE-ERA STYLES FOR HIS COLLECTIONS.

URBAN DECAY EYE SHADOW IN SWF
THIS SHADOW WOULD HAVE BEEN FITTING FOR JANET OR FONDA'S PREVIOUS CHARACTER IN *SINGLE WHITE FEMALE.*

ASTARA BLUE FLAME PURIFICATION MASK
IT MAY NOT HAVE HELPED IN THE BREAST DEPARTMENT (HER SMALL SET WAS A POINT OF CONTENTION WITH HER PIGGISH BOYFRIEND), BUT JANET WAS HAPPY TO SETTLE FOR CLEAR SKIN.

in *Singles*

BRIDGET FONDA

Bridget Fonda's acting gene pool is just too good for her to pursue any other line of work—her dad is Peter Fonda (*Easy Rider*), her aunt is Jane Fonda (*Klute*, *The China Syndrome*), and her grandfather is Henry Fonda (*Twelve Angry Men*, *On Golden Pond*). The freckled, strawberry blonde attended both New York University and the Lee Strasberg Theatre Institute to hone her craft before embarking on a film career. Her moldable, fresh-faced looks caught the attention of Cameron Crowe, who cast her as the lovesick Janet Livermore in *Singles*, his 1992 portrayal of the Seattle grunge scene. The romantic comedy chronicles the lives of a varied group of twenty-somethings living in Seattle and co-stars Matt Dillon, Campbell Scott, and Kyra Sedgwick. Though the film focuses on their troubled relationships, the movie's real highlight is the vibrant music scene it is built around. Crowe threw in cameos from Pearl Jam, Alice in Chains, and Soundgarden, and was supposedly inspired to create this homage to grunge after the untimely death of Andrew Wood, the lead singer of Mother Love Bone. It's tough to decide what's more enticing: the soundtrack or Janet's adorable leather jacket/bowler hat ensemble.

TOO FACED LIP INJECTION
BEFORE SHE TURNED TO SURGICAL MEANS, THIS APTLY NAMED PRODUCT COULD HAVE HELPED PLUMP HER UP.

WET 'N' WILD BLACK EYELINER
IN THE EARLY DAYS OF HOLE, LOVE COULDN'T AFFORD MUCH MORE THAN THIS FAVORITE DRUGSTORE BRAND.

REVLON SUPER LUSTROUS LIPSTICK IN FIRE & ICE
HER SIGNATURE SHADE WAS USUALLY WORN SMEARED ALL OVER HER FACE.

COURTNEY LOVE

Courtney Love toes the line between princess and pariah in the music industry—many a Nirvana fan liken her to Yoko Ono. Shuffled between hippie communes and juvenile halls by her wayward mother, Love was troubled, to say the least. After taking off as a teenager, she spent time in England, Ireland, and Japan, where she worked as a stripper, before landing in Los Angeles in the '80s. After brief turns in both Faith No More and Babes in Toyland, Love founded her own band, Hole, in 1990. Though their first album flopped, her name would soon be met with instant recognition after she married tortured grunge-god Kurt Cobain in 1992—the Nirvana song "Heart-Shaped Box" is about her. The artfully disheveled pair became instant rock royalty, reigning over a kingdom of disaffected youth and producing one child together, Frances Bean. Though their reign would be cut short by Kurt Cobain's tragic suicide in 1994, Love would go on to find her own success, both as Hole's "kinderwhore" (riot grrrl fashion trend of wearing baby-doll dresses plus ripped tights and combat boots attributed by some to Love), and as an actress in films like *The People vs. Larry Flynt* (1996). In recent years, though, Love has gained more notoriety than fame for her questionable parenting techniques, her violent outbursts, and her brash comments—"You're no one in the rock industry unless you've feuded with me or slept with Winona Ryder."

POP BEAUTY GLITTER ADDICT IN RAINBOW EVERY GIRL NEEDS A LITTLE (OR IN RAYANNE'S CASE, A LOT OF) GLITTER IN HER LIFE...EXCEPT, THAT IS, MARIAH.

CHEAP AND CHIC MOSCHINO I LOVE LOVE PERFUMED BATH AND SHOWER GEL RAYANNE WOULD DEFINITELY HAVE STOLEN THIS FRAGRANCE.

STREEKERS TEMPORARY HAIR COLOR BECAUSE HIGHLIGHTS ARE BOOOOORING.

RAYANNE from *My So-Called Life*

A.J. Langer hit her peak in high school—the short-lived, but highly acclaimed cult TV series *My So-Called Life* was her greatest acting gig thus far. Sigh, everything is so much more dramatic when you're a teenager. *My So-Called Life* encapsulated every aspect of teen angst—from the desperate crying sessions to the painful insecurities to the nervous romantic moments—without ever being trite like so many of its prime-time competitors. And while Angela (a Manic-Panicked Claire Danes) may have had a less fractured family, a higher IQ, no drinking problems, and, eventually, Jordan Catalano, it was the unpredictable Rayanne who stole our hearts. Whether she was ditching class, dancing until dawn, engaging in a screaming match with her tarot-card-reading mom, or listening to Angela whine for the umpteenth time about Jordan, Rayanne did it in style. For her, that meant a look that was part rave bunny (minus the pacifier), part ragamuffin, and always a total mess.

SHANNEN DOHERTY

n *Beverly Hills, 90210*

AUSSIE AUSSOME VOLUME MOUSSE-GEL FUSION
BRENDA'S SIGNATURE STRAIGHT CHESTNUT HAIR WAS NEVER STREAKED BLONDE.

COVER GIRL TRUBLEND WHIPPED FOUNDATION
THE CLASSIC TEEN COSMETICS BRAND FOR THE TEEN QUEEN HERSELF.

ANAÏS ANAÏS BY CACHAREL
BRENDA FELT AN AFFINITY FOR ANYTHING FRENCH.

Like it or not, *Beverly Hills, 90210* was a pop-culture phenomenon. Uber-producer Aaron Spelling, the man behind TV success stories like *Charlie's Angels* and *The Love Boat*, created the series in 1990 about spoiled high schoolers living in the most posh of California zip codes to fill a programming gap. Shannen Doherty, fresh from a TV role on *Our House* and parts in the seminal teen films *Girls Just Want To Have Fun* (1985) and *Heathers* (1989), was cast in the lead role of Brenda, opposite Jason Priestley, who played her fraternal twin brother, Brandon. Doherty later revealed that pretending that clean-cut pretty-boy Jason Priestley was her brother was hard because he was "a total babe." Thankfully Brenda had better taste—she only had eyes for motorcycle-riding, bad-boy Dylan with his leather jacket, scruffy face, and scarred eyebrow ("I like your butt...I mean your bike."). Brenda herself was the poster girl for early '90s fashion with her high-waisted tapered Guess? jeans, assortment of cheesy hats, and double-breasted jackets with shoulder pads. But even when she became an exile amongst her bottle-blonde cohorts, and eventually her actual castmates, she was still the best-looking bitch in Beverly Hills.

AVEDA LIP SHINE IN GRAPEFRUIT PULP
"ANYTHING YOU CAN DO TO DRAW ATTENTION TO YOUR MOUTH IS GOOD."

NOXZEMA DAILY CREAM CLEANSER
"OK, SO YOU'RE PROBABLY GOING, 'IS THIS LIKE A NOXZEMA COMMERCIAL OR WHAT?' BUT SERIOUSLY, I HAVE LIKE A WAY NORMAL LIFE FOR A TEENAGE GIRL."

THE BODY SHOP COCOA BUTTER BODY SCRUB
"SOMETIMES YOU HAVE TO SHOW A LITTLE SKIN. THIS REMINDS BOYS OF BEING NAKED AND THEN THEY THINK OF SEX."

ALICIA SILVERSTONE
in *Clueless*

Alicia Silverstone looks like the girl you hated in high school—the pert blonde cheerleader with the perfect smile and curves in all the right places. These natural attributes landed Silverstone her first role (not including the Domino's commercial she did as a child) as a dream-sequence girl on the hit TV series *The Wonder Years*. She was more of a nightmare as the teenage femme-fatale babysitter who seduces an older man in *The Crush* (1993), a hit with the MTV audience. Her tousled blonde hair and naturally pouty lips caught the attention of Aerosmith, who cast Silverstone as the video vixen in "Cryin," "Amazing," and "Crazy," with Liv Tyler, a trilogy that made her the first music-video star. So Silverstone seemed an obvious choice when *Fast Times* alum Amy Heckerling was casting her new movie *Clueless* (1995), a contemporary retelling of Jane Austen's *Emma*. As Cher Horowitz, the pampered California princess, Silverstone discovered a knack for comedy replete with vapid observations—"She's a full-on Monet. Like a painting, see? From far away it's OK, but up close it's a big old mess." Besides influencing fashion trends with her coordinated plaid ensembles and kneesocks, Cher improved the image for Valley girl speak, bringing words like "totally," "whatever," and "as if," into the '90s vernacular.

REVLON COLOR SILK ULTRA LIGHT ASH BLONDE
MALLORY GAVE NEW MEANING TO THE EXPRESSION "BLONDE BOMBSHELL."

M.A.C LIPSTICK IN LADY DANGER
THE NAME PRETTY MUCH SAYS IT ALL.

REDKEN COLOR EXTEND TOTAL COLOR VEIL
EVEN A GIRL ON THE LAM NEEDS TO KEEP HER COLOR LOOKING SHARP.

JULIETTE LEWIS
in *Natural Born Killers*

Juliette Lewis is not the girl next door. She is beloved by audiences and critics alike for her unconventional beauty and uncanny knack for portraying the fragile and the fucked-up—an impressionable, awkward teen in *Cape Fear* (1991), a drifter in *What's Eating Gilbert Grape* (1993), and the naïve girlfriend of a killer in *Kalifornia* (1993). *Natural Born Killers* was no exception. Oliver Stone's explicit 1994 film may have been shocking onscreen, but its premise was respectably principled—the director wanted to expose the manner in which the media sensationalizes crimes and turns killers into celebrities. While his purpose was misunderstood, one fact remains incontrovertible: Juliette Lewis is phenomenal as Mallory. Brutally abused by her lecherous father (played with the appropriate amount of repulsiveness by Rodney Dangerfield), Mallory finds a hero in Mickey Knox (Woody Harrelson), who swoops in and viciously kills her parents but lets her brother live. Leaving one witness to tell the tale becomes the pair's trademark as they crisscross the country on a killing spree, all the while becoming media darlings.

MAKE UP FOR EVER STRASS CRYSTALS
WHETHER IT WAS JUST A BINDI, OR ENTIRE SEMICIRCLES ABOVE HER BROWS, STEFANI WAS ALL ABOUT THE FACE CRYSTALS.

L'ORÉAL FÉRIA EXTRA BLEACH BLONDE
THOUGH HER HAIR WAS POWDER BLUE AND BUBBLEGUM PINK FOR SOME TIME IN THE '90S, SHE ALWAYS WENT BACK TO HER BELOVED BLEACHED BLONDE.

GIORGIO ARMANI ARMANISILK LIPSTICK IN 12
STEFANI IS MOST CERTAINLY NOT ABOUT NUDE COLORS.

GWEN STEFANI in No Doubt

While Gwen Stefani has made a name for herself as a successful solo artist (*Love. Angel. Music. Baby*), actress (*The Aviator*), and fashion designer (LAMB and Harajuku Girls), her original pairing with the members of No Doubt was a bright spot on the '90s music scene. Formed in the late '80s in her hometown of Anaheim, California, with her brother Eric as the original keyboardist (he would drop out to pursue an animation career), Tom Dumont, Adrian Young, and, of course, her former flame Tony Kanal, No Doubt brought SoCal ska to the mainstream. The band had two tepid attempts before hitting it big with 1995's *Tragic Kingdom*, which produced hits like "Don't Speak," "Just a Girl," and "Excuse Me Mr.," and thrust the vivacious, mesmerizing Stefani into the spotlight. The majority of *Tragic Kingdom's* heartfelt songs had been penned by Stefani about the crumbling of her seven-year relationship with fellow band member Kanal, a fact that didn't trouble her for very long because that same year she would meet her future husband, Gavin Rossdale. Though Stefani is still pushing the envelope with her personal style, there was something more authentic about the statements she made, from the Crayola-colored hair and outfits to the outrageous makeup, in the early days of No Doubt.

LAURYN HILL

CAROL'S DAUGHTER LOC BUTTER
HILL'S TINY DREADLOCKS WERE HER SIGNATURE AT THIS TIME.

BURT'S BEES BEESWAX MOISTURIZING CREME
HILL'S SKIN WAS ABSOLUTELY FLAWLESS.

REVLON SUPER LUSTROUS PEARL LIPSTICK IN COFFEE BEAN
WHILE HER MAKEUP CONSTANTLY CHANGED, HER FAVORITE SHADE OF LIPSTICK REMAINED A CREAMY BROWN.

Lauryn Hill's soulful voice defined the latter half of the decade and was featured on two of the '90s' most influential albums: The Fugees' *The Score* (1996) and her first solo effort, *The Miseducation of Lauryn Hill* (1998). Though her stage career began with acting—she appeared briefly on the soap opera *As the World Turns* and opposite Whoopi Goldberg in *Sister Act 2: Back in the Habit*—Hill quickly gravitated toward the mic. *Blunted on Reality* (1994) was the first record by The Fugees (Hill, Pras Michel, and Wyclef Jean), and while it may have been a dud, they were totally redeemed with the now-classic hip-hop album *The Score* (1996), which produced hits like "Killing Me Softly" and "Ready or Not." Hill's melodic voice was the soul of the group, and in 1998, it became the focal point for her solo effort, *The Miseducation of Lauryn Hill*, whose title was drawn from Carter G. Woodson's book, *The Miseducation of the Negro. Miseducation* showed a softer side of Hill, incorporating elements of jazz and R&B, and come Grammy time, broke Carole King's previous record of four awards in one night, earning a total of five. Besides receiving accolades from the music press, Hill was also beloved for her Earth-Mother sense of style—flowing skirts, many all-white ensembles, and a constantly changing array of colorful loose-knit hats—and her natural beauty.

PART

3 THE LOOKS

MAKING FACES

Remember the childhood warning parents love to repeat: if you keep making those mugs, your face will freeze in that position. Well, in the case of the following exquisite faces, "made" by a cross section of the beauty industry's best and brightest makeup artists for *NYLON*, the caveat is less ominous, and downright enticing.

ARIAN FOR M.A.C

JOEY CAMASTA FOR M.A.C

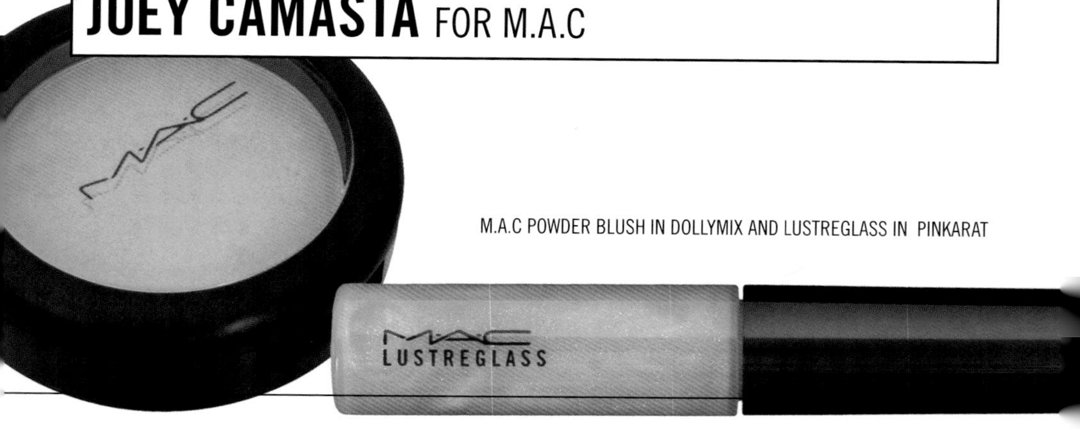

M.A.C POWDER BLUSH IN DOLLYMIX AND LUSTREGLASS IN PINKARAT

"Valley of the Dolls
/ Jean Shrimpton"

KRISTIN GALLEGOS

LAURA MERCIER BRONZING POWDER AND BOURJOIS BLUSH IN CENDRE DE ROSE 48

PATI DUBROFF FOR CHRISTIAN DIOR COSMETICS

"Pure and simple face –this is how I like to wear my makeup..."

DIOR 5 COLOUR EYESHADOW IN MYSTIC JADE AND ADDICT PLASTIC GLOSS #244

JEMMA KIDD

HI-SHINE SILK-TOUCH LIP GLOSS IN BARE AND
EYE WARDROBE EYE SHADOW QUARTET IN GREY

"Technicolor Inspiration."

JULIE TOMLINSON

SHU UEMURA PRESSED EYESHADOW TURQUOISE #302
AND M.A.C LIPGLASS IN SPITE

"1920s Inspiration."

NARS DUO EYESHADOWS IN DEMON LOVER AND PARIS AND GIORGIO ARMANI BLACK KOHL EYELINER

GINA BROOKE FOR SHU UEMURA

SHU UEMURA LIQUID BLACK LINER AND LOLISHINE ROUGE 335 LIPSTICK

SARA GLICK

"Inspiration: Marc Jacobs 2006 Ready to Wear"

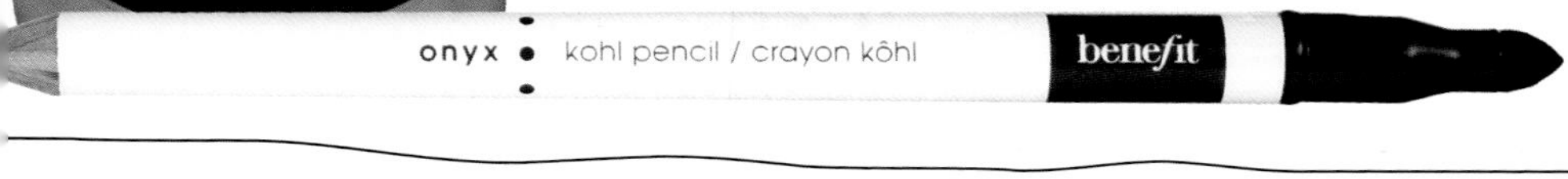

BY TERRY ECLAT DE PERLE #1 AND BENEFIT SKETCHING EYE PENCIL IN ONYX

GORDON ESPINET FOR M.A.C

M.A.C LIP PENCIL IN MAGENTA AND LIPSTICK IN UP THE AMP

MALLY RONCAL

Old Hollywood glamour with a little modern love.”

MALLY BEAUTY XTRA HOLD MAXIMIZING MASCARA AND LIPSTICK IN WILD ORCHID

"Gitane."

VINCENT LONGO

VINCENT LONGO WET DIAMOND EYESHADOW IN DAWN FLESH AND EYESHADOW TRIO IN CURIOUS VIOLET, AND SATIN PLUM EYE PENCIL

LINDA CANTELLO

FOR YVES SAINT LAURENT

YSL ROUGE PUR LIPSTICK IN NO.19

the peekaboo wave

There are actresses who are remembered more for alluring aspects of their personal appearance than for their thespian talents. Veronica Lake, whom Bette Davis once bitterly referred to as "the most beautiful person who ever came to Hollywood," was one such actress. Despite star turns in a series of excellent film noirs, Lake is most well-known for her wavy, side-parted hairstyle and peekaboo bangs. As the story goes, while shooting publicity photos for *40 Little Mothers* (1940), a thick strand of hair kept tumbling over her face, and so began the peekaboo trend. In fact, the look became so popular during the World War II era that Lake had to record public service announcements warning women to tie back their peekaboos while operating machinery, due to a number of on-the-job accidents involving hair becoming ensnared. The style, which is created with a wide-barrel curling iron and can employ soft waves or the more angular Marcel waves, courtesy of hairdresser Marcel Grateau, oozes feminine sex appeal, and its allure has endured for generations.

mohawk

If each hairstyle had a comic book text bubble hovering above it, the Mohawk's would hold two words: Fuck You. If the braid is a peace sign, the Mohawk is the middle finger. Thought to have been worn by indigenous tribes in the Great Lakes region during times of war, this aggressive style was resurrected by members of London's and New York's '70s punk movements as the perfect complement to the antiestablishment look and sound exemplified by bands like the Plasmatics, the Sex Pistols, the Ramones, and the Clash. The stiff, upright style was achieved through laborious effort—often sculpted and molded by hand, it was held in place with a mixture of ingredients like hair gel, egg whites, Elmer's glue, corn starch, and gelatin. The variations on the traditional crown-to-nape fan shape were endless: there were the liberty spikes, which spread outward like those of Lady Liberty; a Mohawk called the "devilock" that drooped across the forehead; and the "dreadhawk," which merged dreadlocks and spikes in an unlikely marriage of punk and hippie 'dos. The millennial-edition faux-hawk is more vanilla than its counterculture originator, gracing the heads of MTV's wimpy mall-punk bands and, more attractively, Angelina Jolie's son, Maddox.

bouffant

The word "bouffant" calls to mind a few things: grandmothers in Boca, cotillion ceremonies, and John Waters characters (*Hairspray*, anyone?). But while the bouffant may be old-fashioned, it most certainly does not have to look old. Derived from the French word *bouffer*, meaning "to puff or puff out," the full-figured style is often credited to hairdresser Michael Kazan and reached the peak of its popularity in the '50s and early '60s. A combination of mesh hair rollers (or empty clean juice cans), strong hold hairspray, piles of bobby pins, and a lot of backcombing were employed to achieve the desired volume. The most voluminous result was the beehive, the bouffant's larger, more rigid cousin, popularized by singers like Martha and the Vandellas, actress Barbara Eden, and most recently the B-52s. But it's the simpler, tousled, upswept bouffant, modeled best by the permanently pouty Brigitte Bardot (hers, created by French stylist Jacques Dessange, was called the *choucroute*) that has stood the test of time, looking just as fresh and sexy now as it did half a century ago.

pixie

pixie, n. : a fairylike or elfin creature, especially one that is mischievous; a playful sprite

When the "living legend of hair," Vidal Sassoon, shaped Mia Farrow's golden locks into a dramatic pixie cut during the filming of Polanski's frightful 1968 film *Rosemary's Baby*, perhaps it was this definition that he had in mind. Sassoon's resulting symmetrical style transformed Farrow from a dime-a-dozen pert blonde to an ethereal stunner tiptoeing around androgyny. But the pixie's not for everybody—to really pull off this ultra-gamine look, you need both confidence and beauty. In Farrow's time, Twiggy followed suit, and, in recent years, petite-featured actresses like Winona Ryder and Natalie Portman have sported the closely-shorn cut. But while the pixie may negate the need for your blow-dryer and a stack of grooming products, it does require many salon visits to maintain the wispy layers.

bob

Ever wonder what hairstyle a pop-culture provocateur like Madonna might have sported had she been around in the '20s? It would have surely been the ultra-risqué bob. Invented in 1909 by the acclaimed French hairdresser Antoine, the cut was inspired by the ultimate female rebel, Miss Joan of Arc. The bob gained worldwide fame when silent screen star Louise Brooks made the cut. Hers was a "Buster Brown" or "Dutch Boy," meaning it was short and slick with straight bangs and face-skimming sides, and was referred to by some as the "black helmet." Other variations included the "Eton Crop," which was even shorter, and ones that added *croche couers*, spit curls set either on the forehead or in front of the ears. But it wasn't the ultra-short length that scandalized so much as the contentious behaviors like smoking, drinking, sex, and fast-paced dancing that were associated with it. Hence, the bob became a historical landmark—a visible indicator of social changes and the ultimate reflection of women's coming into their own.

the afro

It was a combination of panache and politics that earned the Afro widespread popularity. The Black Pride and Civil Rights movements were gaining momentum amidst the already turbulent political atmosphere of the '60s, and many African-Americans were seeking ways to embrace their heritage. "Black is Beautiful" was the movement's slogan, and the Afro, from the word Afro-American, was its signature style. The oversized, thick, tautly curled halo was hair in its most natural state, and the once-popular harsh chemical straighteners and machines were rejected because they reinforced "white" standards of beauty. Activist Angela Davis personified the style's political roots; blaxploitation film star Pam Grier, whose bad-ass characters were known for hiding weapons in their curls, sported a 'fro, along with musicians like Jimi Hendrix, the Jackson 5, and the Supremes. Hair companies, always ready to profit from a trend no matter where it comes from, began to market products and tools, like the pick, specifically for Afro maintenance. Though the style may no longer be just a badge of racial pride, the Afro remains a statement.

feathered shag

There are cuts that are simply admired, and then there are ones that inspire and are emulated by legions of women, over and over again. Farrah Fawcett's famously feathered shag, created by stylist José Eber and alternately referred to as the "Farrah Flip" and the "wingback," was that cut—during the '70s and early '80s many millions of women played copycat. Deemed by *Time* magazine as "the epitome of '70s glamour," the bouncy, layered look was demonstrated best by Fawcett on the notoriously nipply red-swimsuit cheesecake poster that hung in many a teenage boy's bedroom during that decade. But though the Angels eventually went off the air, the cut had a major early-'90s comeback when *Friends* came along. And though it's still around, nowadays, thanks to the use of the razor's edge, it's more rough than Rachel.

bangs

Bangs, the requisite component of many a young girl's haircut, can easily evoke the same youthful quality far into adulthood. A fringe, as it's called in Europe, has been around since the ancient Egyptians and Greeks cut their hair in heavy, straight lines across the forehead. The Middle Ages saw a number of women sporting bangs that hovered extremely close to the hairline, and they even flirted with controversy for a brief period in the 1600s, when men-of-the-cloth believed they were a worrisome sign of vanity. From the short, frizzy "Alexandra fringe" popularized by Princess Alexandra of Wales in the late 1800s, to Liza Minelli's Goth-like V-shape, to the coquettish minis of Bettie Page, bangs have cloaked some of the most distinctive faces. But it's Jane Birkin's '60s-era eye-grazing fringe that really inspires admiration…from both Monsieur Serge and scores of women.

the blonde

Two blondes are walking in a forest when they spot a pair of tracks. One suggests they're bear tracks, while the other says they're fox tracks. Then they get hit by a train.

Turns out that the dumb blonde concept does have, er, roots. Allegedly, in the late 1700s, there lived a flaxen-haired French courtesan by the name of Rosalie Duth who was so famous for her scatterbrained ways that she was satirized in a play called *Les Curiosités de la Foire* (1775). And thus, the blonde joke was born. While Marilyn Monroe was not the original blonde bombshell—that honor belongs to Monroe's childhood idol Jean Harlow—her enduring legacy as an international pop-culture phenomenon makes her the most iconic one. But not all blondes are created equal, at least according to esteemed anthropologist Grant McCracken, who created, in his 1995 book *Big Hair: A Journey into the Transformation of Self*, a "blondeness periodic table." The six categories include: the bombshell blonde (Marilyn, Mae West), the sunny blonde (Goldie Hawn), the brassy blonde (Debbie Harry), the dangerous blonde (Sharon Stone), the society blonde (Nan Kempner), and the cool blonde (Marlene Dietrich). And though fewer than twenty-five percent of women who are born blonde retain the color past their teenage years, it is a shade that many, through the application of various bleaching agents, will flirt with at some point in their life, if only to determine whether or not there's any truth to the old adage "blondes have more fun."

SHOPPING LIST

BEAUTY SHOPS Around The Globe

NEW YORK CITY

AEDES DE VENUSTAS, 9 Christopher Street, 212.206.8674, aedes.com
ALCONE BEAUTY CLUB, 235 West 19th Street, 212.633.0551
CO BIGELOW, 414 Avenue of the Americas, 212.533.2732, bigelowchemists.com
LAFCO, 285 Lafayette Street, 212.925.0001, lafcony.com
PHARMA, 17 Clinton Street, 212.505.3505, pharmanyc.com
RICKY'S, Multiple locations, rickysnyc.com
TAKASHIMAYA, 693 Fifth Avenue, 212.350.0100, ny-takashimaya.com
ZITOMER, 969 Madison Avenue, 212.737.5560, zitomer.com

LOS ANGELES

KALOLOGIE, 132 S. Robertson Blvd, 310.276.9670, kalologie.com
LARCHMONT BEAUTY CENTER, 208 N. Larchmont Blvd, 323.461.0162, larchmontbeauty.com
LE PINK, 1545 Echo Park Avenue, 213.250.0265
NUMBER ONE BEAUTY SUPPLY, 1426 Montana Avenue, Santa Monica, 310.656.2455
PALMETTO, 8321 West Third Street, 323.653.2470

LONDON

BOOTS THE CHEMIST, Multiple locations, boots.com
SCREENFACE, 48 Monmouth Street, +44 20.7836.3955
SPACE NK, 127-131 Westbourne Grove, +44 20.7727.8063
THE ORGANIC PHARMACY, 169 Kensington High Street, +44 20.7351.2232, theorganicpharmacy.com
ZARVIS, 4 Portobello Green, 281 Portobello Road, +44 20.8968.5435, zarvis.com

PARIS

COLETTE, 213 rue Saint-Honore, +33 1.55.35.33.90, colette.fr
DETAILLE 1905, 10 rue Saint-Lazare, +33 1.48.78.68.50, detaille.com
GALERIE NOEMIE, 17 rue du Cygne, +33 1.44.76.06.26, galerienoemie.com
MAKI, 9 rue Mansart, 0142813376
MONOPRIX, Multiple locations

HONG KONG AND TOKYO

HYAKU-SUKE, 2-2-14 Asakusa, Tokyo, +81 3.3841.7058
ISETAN, 3-14-1 Shinjuku, Tokyo, +81 3.3352.1111
JOYCE, 16 Queen's Road, New World Tower, Hong Kong, +852 2810.1120
LANE CRAWFORD, Multiple locations, lanecrawford.com

ROME AND MILAN

10 CORSO COMO, Corso Como 10, Milan, +39 02.65.35.37
LIMONI BEST, Galleria del Corso 4, Milan, +39 02.78.37.85
MATEROZZOLI, Piazza San Lorenzo, Lucina 5, Rome, +39 06.68.89.26.86
ROMA STORE, Via della Lungaretta 63, Rome, +39 06.58.18.789

WEBSITES

ACQUA DI PARMA, neimanmarcus.com and bergdorfgoodman.com
AGENT PROVOCATEUR, at agent provocateur stores
ALMAY, at drugstores
ANAIS ANAIS BY CACHAREL, at amazon.com
ANNA SUI, victoria secret stores, anna sui boutiques
ASTARA, exhalespa.com, astaraskincare.com
AUSSIE, at drugstores
AVEDA, aveda.com
AWAKE, at beauty.com
BARE ESCENTUALS, bareescentuals.com
BENEFIT, benefitcosmetics.com
BÉSAME, besamecosmetics.com and henri bendel, nyc
BIOTHERM, biotherm-usa.com
BLISS, blissworld.com
BOBBI BROWN, bobbibrown.com
BODY SHOP, thebodyshop.com
BOND NO. 9, at bond no. 9 boutiques and saks fifth avenue
BOUCHERON, saks fifth avenue, bloomingdales
BOURJOIS, sephora.com
BUMBLE AND BUMBLE, find stores at bumbleandbumble.com
BURT'S BEES, burtsbees.com
BVLGARI, neiman marcus, saks fifth avenue
BY TERRY, at barney's new york
CALVIN KLEIN, at macy's stores or macys.com
CAROL'S DAUGHTER, carolsdaughter.com
CAROLINA HERRERA, at department stores
CARON, 1-877-88-CARON
CARTIER, at cartier boutiques nationwide
CHANEL, chanel.com, saks fifth avenue
CHRISTIAN BRETON, at henri bendel, nyc
CHRISTIAN DIOR, at fine department stores
CLAIROL, at drugstores
CLARINS, clarins.com
CLINIQUE, at department stores
CONAIR, conair.com, 1-800-3-CONAIR
COVER GIRL, at drugstores
CREST, at drugstores
DARPHIN, at neiman marcus
DAVINES, davines.com, 1-866-328-4637
DELUX BEAUTY, deluxbeauty.com
DERMALOGICA, dermalogica.com
DIANNE BRILL, beautyhabit.com, la petite coquette
DOLCE & GABBANA, at fine department stores
DOVE, at drugstores
DR. BRANDT, sephora.com, nordstrom
DR. HAUSCHKA, drhauschka.com
DUWOP, duwop.com
EASY STRAIGHT, easystraight.com

ELIZABETH ARDEN, elizabetharden.com, dillards.com
ELIZABETH TAYLOR, at department stores
ESTEE LAUDER, esteelauder.com, and bloomingdales
FACE STOCKHOLM, 888-334-FACE, facestockholm.com
FREDERIC FEKKAI, at frederic fekkai salons and spas, and neiman marcus
FRESH, fresh.com
GARNIER, at drugstores
GIORGIO ARMANI, giorgioarmanibeauty.com
GIVENCHY, at select saks fifth avenue stores and saks.com
GO SMILE, gosmile.com, sephora stores
GOLDIE, bath and body works or bbw.com
GOODY, at drugstores
GUERLAIN, at neiman marcus stores
HARD CANDY, hardcandy.com
JEAN PAUL GAULTIER, at fine department and specialty stores
JEMMA KIDD MAKE UP SCHOOL, neimanmarcus.com and bergdorfgoodman.com
JERGENS, at drugstores
JO MALONE, jomalone.com, neiman marcus
JOHN FRIEDA, at drugstores
JOY BY JEAN PATOU, at fine department stores
JULIE HEWETT, juliehewett.net
KERASTASE, call 877.748.8357 for salon locations
KEVYN AUCOIN, kevynaucoin.com
KIEHL'S, kiehls.com
LANCÔME, lancome.com
LANVIN, saks fifth avenue
LAURA MERCIER, lauramercier.com
LOLA, lolacosmetics.com
LORAC, beauty.com, and sephora stores
L'OCCITANE, usa.loccitane.com
L'OREAL, at drugstores
LOVE'S BABY SOFT, at amazon.com
M.A.C, maccosmetics.com
MANIC PANIC, spencer gifts and hot topic stores
MAKE UP FOR EVER, make up forever boutique, soho nyc
MALLY BEAUTY, qvc.com and henri bendel, nyc
MARC JACOBS, saks fifth avenue, marc jacobs boutiques
MATRIX, matrix.com
MAX FACTOR, at walmart stores
MAYBELLINE NEW YORK, at drugstores
MICHAEL KORS, sephora stores, nordstrom
MODELCO, at select sephora and victoria's secret stores
MOSCHINO, sephora.com
MURAD, murad.com
NAIR, at drugstores
NARS, narscosmetics.com
NEUTROGENA, at drugstores
NINA RICCI, at department stores
NOXZEMA, at drugstores
OIL OF OLAY, at drugstores
O.P.I, opi.com
ORIGINS, origins.com, and origins retail stores
PANTENE, at drugstores
PAUL LABRECQUE, paullabrecque.com
PAUL MITCHELL, paulmitchell.com
PHILOSOPHY, philosophy.com
PHYTO, 1-800-55PHYTO, sephora.com
PLAYBOY COSMETICS, playboybeauty.com
POP BEAUTY, sephora.com
POUT, victoriassecret.com
PRADA, neiman marcus stores
PRESCRIPTIVES, prescriptives.com
RED FLOWER, at barney's new york and redflower.com
REDKEN, 1-800-REDKEN-8, redken.com
REVLON, at drugstores
RIMMEL, at drugstores
ROBERT PIGUET, sephora.com
SEPHORA, at sephora stores
SHISEIDO, shiseido.com
SHU UEMURA, shuuemura.com
SMASHBOX, at Nordstrom and smashbox.com
STELLA MCCARTNEY, sephora stores and nordstrom
STILA, sephora and stilacosmetics.com
STREEKERS, streekers.com
TARTE, tartecosmetics.com, and select sephora stores
THIERRY MUGLER, clarins.com, and nordstrom
T3, t3tourmaline.com
THREE CUSTOM COLOR SPECIALISTS, threecustom.com and beauty.com
TOO FACED, sephora.com
TRESEMMÉ, at drugstores
URBAN DECAY, at sephora and urbandecay.com
VERSACE, at Versace boutiques nationwide
VICTORIA'S SECRET, victoriassecret.com
VINCENT LONGO, at sephora stores and victoriassecret.com
VO5, at drugstores
WET 'N' WILD, at drugstores
YVES SAINT LAURENT, at fine department stores

CREDITS

PHOTOGRAPHY

MARK ABRAHAMS
pages 4, 7

ALEX ANTITCH
page 40

GUY AROCH
pages 12, 13, 70, 208

ANETTE AURELL
page 49

BLOSSOM BERKOFSKY
pages 18, 21, 207

XAVIER BRUNET
page 24

FABIO CHIZZOLA
page 141

CLANG
pages 6, 74

ALAN CLARKE
pages 9, 35

ELIZABET DAVISDOTTIR
pages 8, 157, 215

ROBERT ERDMANN
pages 14, 42, 43

FUTURE PLANET OF STYLE
pages 10, 11, 53

MARK WIMBERLY & RADEK GROSMAN
page 204

RICK HAYLOR
page 59

NICK HAYMES
page 73

SPRAGUE HOLLANDER
page 54

ULI HOLTZ
page 203

MARVIN SCOTT JARRETT
pages 3, 17, 26, 30, 67, 168, 212

JOSHUA JORDAN
page 38

RICHARD KERN
page 5

MARCELLO KRASILCIC
page 104

DUC LAIO
page 36

ALASDAIR MCLELLAN
page 199

JASON NOCITO
pages 56, 213

FRED RAMBAUD
pages 44, 126

MARY ROZZI
pages 50, 85

ILAN RUBIN
pages 82, 196

FRANK SCHWERE
page 29

PATRIC SHAW
page 200

TINA TYRELL
pages 65, 211

PRIVATE ICONS
COURTESY OF THE EVERETT COLLECTION
pages 86-103, 106-125, 130-139, 142, 143, 146,147, 152-154, 158, 159, 161, 162-167, 170-172, 174-177, 179

HENRY DILTZ / CORBIS
pages 128

JOE GIRON / CORBIS
pages 178

HULTON-DEUTCH COLLECTION / CORBIS
page 145

NEAL PRESTON / CORBIS
page 151

SYGMA / CORBIS
page 173

STILL LIFE PHOTOGRAPHY
CHIKA KOBARI

COVER
MARVIN SCOTT JARRETT

BACK COVER
BLOSSOM BERKOFSKY

ILLUSTRATION

JOSH GURRIE
pages 28, 31, 32, 37, 39, 41, 45, 51, 55, 58, 61, 64, 72, 75, 148, 155, 160, 201, 202

JENNY MÖRTSELL / FAMILY
pages 27, 33, 34, 66, 69, 79, 198, 206, 210

EUGENIA TSIMIKLIS
pages 47, 48, 52, 63, 76, 77

REBECCA WETZLER
pages 42, 46, 53, 57, 71, 207, 209, 214

CREDITS

FIORELLA VALDESOLO WOULD LIKE TO THANK

MICHAEL EDWARDS
HOLLY SIEGEL
MARY CLARKE
KARA JESELLA
JESSALYNN KELLER
APRIL LONG
ROSEMARY RODRIGUEZ
JULIA SLOAN
SARA SKIRBOLL
STEPHANIE HUANG
LIZ FRIEDLAND
CLAIRE BANDEL
ERIN HAMILTON
JOY-LEE PASQUALONI
PATRICIA DENTE
RACHAEL KELLEY
RUTHIE VEXLER
KIRSTEN NEWMAN
CARRAN AUWERTER
ELIZABETH RILEY
EMILY SHAPOFF
MARQUITA FLADGER
FRANNY VIOLA
JACQUELINE BAETIONG
FRANCA GERRARD
KATHERINE GODON
TRANDA MISINI
TARA EISENBERG
ROSE PILATO
MAX BONBREST
SUZANNE STAGL
ALISON HALJUN
CORINNE ZADIGAN
CATHY O'BRIEN
PATI DUBROFF
SARAH GLICK
DARIAN
MALLY RONCAL
VINCENT LONGO
GORDON ESPINET
JULIE TOMLINSON
JEMMA KIDD
KRISTIN GALLEGOS
JOEY CAMASTA
GORDON ESPINET
LINDA CANTELLO
FRIENDS, FAMILY & NATE

SPECIAL THANKS TO

MARVIN SCOTT JARRETT
JACLYNN JARRETT
FIORELLA VALDESOLO
HEATHER CATANIA
STACEY MARK
JOSH GURRIE
HUONG PHAM
CHIKA KOBARI
WINONA BARTON-BALLENTINE
MICHAEL PANGILINAN
CHARLES MIERS
ELLEN NIDY
SUSAN HOSMER
ALLISON WILLIAMS
CAITLIN LEFFEL
KAIJA MARKOE
UNIVERSE PUBLISHING
THE EVERETT COLLECTION
CORBIS